# Raves
## for *Lifeness*

"**Tom Rubens is the real thing**—an entrepreneur who knows what it's like to try and then fail, to try and then win, and, through it all, to pour your passion, your integrity, and your singular, incomparable life into whatever you do. He cares about business, but most of all he cares about bringing your *life* to your business. This book is a testament to it all."

> —Trebbe Johnson Author of *The World is a Waiting Lover*

"*Lifeness* is a book that speaks directly to the issues facing every entrepreneur. Whether you are the founder of a multi-billion-dollar startup, or thinking about quitting your job to open a landscaping business, **Tom's stories of success and failure, both business and personal, will illuminate the path for the next step on your journey**."

> —Dr. Ivan Misner, NY Times bestselling author and Founder of BNI

"In one evening immersed in his fables—stories of life considered, of learning and failure, love and focus, risk and the great forces that move in human relationships—I found **Tom Rubens' message of harmonious living poured into my brain pan like hot, liquid understanding**."

> —Robert Downey, Founding Partner International Risk Consultants

"**A wonderful, inspirational and in the best meaning of the word, useful, guide for entrepreneurs**—grounded in one man's real-life experiences, successes, failures and ongoing development as a man, father, entrepreneur and human being."

> —Reggie Mara, Author, Poet, Creative Director and core faculty at Teleosis Institute

# LIFENESS

HARMONIZE AN ENTREPRENEURIAL LIFE

TOM RUBENS

BSB PUBLISHING

*For my favorite human being, Sam Rubens.*
*I have no idea why God chose me to be your father,*
*but your love has been my light since the day you were born.*
*I love you, Buddy.*

# CONTENTS

*If greatness should ever accidentally stumble upon you,*
*let it catch you hard at work.*

—Elizabeth Gilbert

# INTRODUCTION

I LIKE MAKING UP WORDS to describe things, and I thought I had come up with a pretty good one as the title for this book by combining the words "life" and "business." Not exactly genius, but it fit perfectly with my message here. Unfortunately, a simple Google search burst my bubble. It turns out that "lifeness" is actually a word, albeit a pretty obscure one. My *Pocket Oxford* doesn't list it, but Wiktionary gives the following definition:

**lifeness:** *noun*
The state or quality of having a life.

So, the word exists, but my new usage is not part of the definition. Let's change that right now. Henceforth, the primary definition shall be:

The state or quality of having a life in which personal and business goals are harmoniously merged to maximize the joy and abundance derived from each.

This is not another "how to" book. It will not delineate "the three things you absolutely need to know to find the pot of gold at the end of the rainbow," nor is it a motivational or "self-help" book. I'm neither a guru nor the guardian of the answer to the Final Jeopardy Question. Rather, this book is a collection of moments and revelations from my own life, some of which occurred quietly and some that were more disruptive. In these stories, I hope you will see your own truth. After all, it is through hearing other people's stories that we learn, heal, and gain awareness. This is a book that—if I have achieved my goal in writing it—will ignite your awareness of your own potential *lifeness*, and inspire you to set forth on a path toward harmonizing your personal and business goals.

During over forty years as an entrepreneur, I've figured out ways to make money beyond drawing a paycheck as an employee. Chronologically, after graduating from college, I traded commodities and options on the floors of the Chicago Board Options Exchange, The Chicago Board of Trade, and The Chicago Mercantile Exchange. Next, I owned and operated Minor League Basketball and Baseball teams in Michigan, Iowa, and Illinois. Then, I founded a real estate brokerage firm in Dayton. After representing thousands of buyers and sellers and opening satellite offices in Cincinnati and Chicago, I sold that business and began my coaching career.

Not every endeavor will make my "Greatest Hits" album. Though it may seem counterintuitive, much of what I've learned about running a successful business has come from experiences in the wilderness, far from any corporate office or strategic planning session. Conversely, the study of corporate culture has taught me how to be a better father, friend, and husband.

In business, numbers are important. Measuring profit and loss is how we keep score. As a business coach, my job is to help my clients maximize the monetary value of their businesses. So of course I examine balance sheets and profit-and-loss statements. The financial success of a business is my foremost concern. Yet what is the value of abundant wealth if it comes at the cost of a fulfilling life?

Perhaps, as mine once was, your livelihood is sucking the life right out of you. You long to be more effective in business and more fulfilled in your personal life. If so, this book was written for you.

The inspiration to write this book arose from my unshakable belief that entrepreneurial success and a joyful personal life are achievable only through the intentional alignment of the business culture you create and the personal core values you practice with your family and friends.

The core messages of the stories you are about to read— accompanied by occasional nuggets of advice—are a vital part of my practice and how I show up in the world. I gauge my success by the degree to which my clients are able to harmoniously integrate their business plans with the plans they have for their lives. If you're able see yourself in some of my stories and begin to make the necessary course corrections to align your business and your life, I've accomplished my mission.

The mother of a dear friend used to say that a child's first form of prayer is to wonder. Creating a remarkable *lifeness*, begins with wonder. As you read this book, allow yourself to wonder how you will feel when you take full responsibility for your reactions to the people and events in your life. Wonder what it will take for your business and personal lives to merge harmoniously.

Joseph Campbell famously said, "Your life is the fruit of your own doing." I hope this book nurtures the seeds you've already planted and helps you find a harmonious path toward an abundant life.

# 1

# ANYTHING'S POSSIBLE

*The only person you are destined to become*
*is the person you decide to be.*
—Ralph Waldo Emerson

I LOVE MY WORK. TRULY. I am privileged to be able to help entrepreneurs transform their businesses and their lives by giving them the tools they need to succeed. I get to read books that move me, study with people who inspire me, and write words that bring me joy. I am a lucky and grateful man.

I haven't always been able to say that.

A few years ago, I was miserable and dreaded going to work in the morning. I was in a perpetual bad mood, just a tick away from exploding in a violent rage, and my business and personal life suffered from the toxic energy that I carried with me everywhere. I didn't want to be in my own presence. I felt trapped and couldn't see a way out.

At that time, I owned a real estate brokerage firm, and my primary clients were the biggest and best-known players in the mortgage loan crisis. I listed and sold hundreds of foreclosed properties yearly. My days were spent speaking with distressed people who had lost their homes, overwhelmed asset managers (employees responsible for overseeing the disposition and sale of thousands of foreclosed properties) drunk on the power that came with their sudden dominance of the real estate landscape, and investors aiming to profit from the misfortune of others.

I felt as if I was under attack from all sides. Homeowners viewed me as the representative of the Great Satan removing them from their homes. All the rage and frustration they felt toward the system was spewed in my direction. And, as starving traditional real estate agents saw the value in becoming "foreclosure specialists," asset managers went from dateless wallflowers to the belles of the ball. Buried under a mountain of regulations and paperwork, they took great joy in pointing to the onslaught of suitors as an excuse for treating their longstanding relationships with loyal agents as fully disposable.

The increased supply of foreclosed property begat overcrowded seminars promising easy and instant wealth creation in the previously sleepy "flipping" category, and the result was a feeding frenzy of naïve investors expecting to "steal" every house they saw. In their minds, the only thing that stood between them and colossal wealth was a listing agent—like me—with a different opinion of the value regarding the wannabe mogul's latest targeted property.

Away from the office, my personal life was a mess. My romantic relationships were empty and brief, and I was gradually disconnecting from my dearest friends. When I answered the phone with my son, Sam, in the car, he would look at me and say, "Try to be nice now, Daddy." I couldn't have been living less harmoniously.

Wow! Just typing those words brings back the heaviness I felt back then. Got *lifeness*? Not exactly.

I was stuck in full-on victim mode. I hated my life and contaminated everyone in my office. Rudeness and anger were my default responses to anyone who crossed my path. Of course, everyone else was the problem. Poor me.

In retrospect, I'm ashamed of how toxic my behavior was at that time. I thought the deep spiritual work I'd done over the previous decade had exorcised the victim energy that was once my constant companion, but the foundational growth I had achieved was perilously close to crumbling in the face of my unchecked anger.

Life inside my head was getting really dark.

Late one night, headed home in a driving rainstorm after another miserable day at the office, I felt overwhelmed with anger toward one of my clients. She was a key employee at one of the largest sellers of distressed properties in the country, and all I could think of was how much I wanted her to disappear.

I was losing control of myself and I couldn't see a way to turn down the volume on my fury.

My internal raging was interrupted by a thought of Sam, and a conversation we'd had a couple years earlier. Sam is autistic, and he and I had a ritual that began as my way of encouraging him to believe in his own ability to achieve great things. I would greet him in the morning with a hug and say in his ear, "Anything's possible."

He would then say the same thing back to me in an "Okay, Dad, I'll say this 'cause you want me to" sort of way.

One morning, he made a subtle change in his response. This time he said, "Anything's possible, Daddy." Whoa. Where did that come from? Now he was telling me something, not the other way around. I instantly got the message.

Anything is possible, including changing my perspective.

Could I do that now, filled with rage as I was toward someone who controlled a significant percentage of my income?

I thought my work was killing my spirit. I derived no joy from my business. It was strictly a revenue source, and the cost was eating me alive. Reliving that moment with Sam took me back to the lesson he'd taught me and that I'd forgotten in my downward spiral. I realized that the business itself was not dark and depressing—that was just how I had chosen to see it. I knew many people in the default industry who led happy and productive lives. They focused on being of service to their clients, their community, and their employees. Their work brought them joy, and they had loving families. The same work that was overwhelming me with venom brought them happiness and fulfillment.

I didn't have to be angry all the time. I didn't have to consume the negativity sent in my direction; it wasn't meant for me, anyway. I had allowed myself to become collateral damage, caught in the crossfire of someone else's story, but I didn't have to take it personally. Instead, I could choose to harmonize.

Anything's possible.

My life began to shift when I acknowledged that I was stuck in a dreary world of my own creation. I set a goal of selling the business within eighteen months. Simply envisioning the end, loosened the noose. Looking for a solution to my problem rather than acting the victim empowered me. As I opened myself to possibility, I realized there was a willing buyer right in front of me.

Stuck in my personal bubble of negativity, I had been totally unaware of the impact I was having on my staff. It had been readily apparent to them that the business was headed for disaster, and my once-loyal team had been preparing to jump ship before it exploded. When I mentioned to my strongest agent that I was hoping to get out, he told me he believed that he could reenergize the team and steer the ship to greater success than we had ever enjoyed under my leadership. We quickly came to an agreement, and I turned in my office keys less than six weeks later. Selling that business led me to where I am today.

After taking a few months off to decompress, I focused on the next chapter of my business life. I made a list including my greatest strengths—the ability to listen to, inspire, and guide others—and the skills I most enjoyed using: one-to-one communication, writing, and teaching. Then, I made a list of non-negotiables:

- Work from home
- No employees
- Low overhead
- Freedom to control my schedule

Five years later, I have a thriving coaching practice, doing work I thoroughly enjoy with clients who drive me to play bigger every day. You're reading my first book, and my second book, the companion *Lifeness Journal*, was released simultaneously. My third book is outlined and will be released next year.

My personal life has gone from being a vast wasteland to containing the deepest, most meaningful relationship I've ever known. I get to wake up each morning and share my life with a woman whose love and compassion inspire me to reach for the highest fruit in all aspects of my life. Trish and Sam conspire to make every day a new present I get to joyfully unwrap.

Yep. *Anything's possible, Daddy.*

# AROUND THE BASES WITH
# AN ENTREPRENEUR

*Our job in this lifetime is not to fit*
*into some mold that others have determined*
*is best for us. Our job is to find out who we*
*already are, and become it.*
—Steven Pressfield

I GREW UP IN A typical suburban town, before color TV, when the notion of chaining your bike to a metal rack in front of your school would have been totally absurd. We didn't have organized sports, so we'd just call our friends and get together on Saturdays and after school to play baseball, football, hockey—whatever sport was in season.

When I was in sixth grade, my school district formed a softball league. Each of the four local grammar schools fielded a team and played each other at the local ballpark on Saturdays.

I wasn't a great athlete, but I was a guy you wanted on your team because I just hated to lose. I would do whatever it took to avoid the bitter taste of defeat. I like to think I brought a passion to the game that my pals admired.

One Saturday, early in our season, I stepped up to the plate just hoping to make solid contact. I wasn't much of a hitter, but I could run fast, and all I needed was to put the ball in play to have a chance to get on base.

This time, I exceeded my expectations. I crushed the ball into the gap in right center and had delusions of grandeur as I dropped my bat and began my sprint around the bases.

I was overwhelmed with excitement and awe at the power my bat had generated. As I rounded first, the right fielder was still chasing the ball.

By the time I got to second, the right fielder had picked up the ball and relayed it to the second baseman, who had run out into short right field to take the throw. I decided to stretch this clean double into a triple. I figured my chances were pretty good; we were only twelve-year-olds, and if you've ever watched kids play softball, you know that errors are more common than great catches and strong, accurate throws.

About halfway to third, I realized I was in trouble. The third baseman, with ball in glove, was waiting for me, poised to make the tag. In that instant, in that split-second when I passed the shortstop, I realized I had a decision to make. I could stop, head back to second, and hope to somehow avoid getting caught in a rundown. Or I could keep heading for third and attempt to elude the tag.

With my mind and body racing at full speed, I thought about Jimmy Goldstein, the third baseman. I knew him from summer camp, and there was one key piece of information that sealed my decision to go for third rather than run back to second. Jimmy was a crier. He was an excellent ballplayer, but quick to cry when he so much as scraped his knee. I went for a hard slide, with my foot aimed at Jimmy's mitt. I counted on him dropping the ball and crying as soon as I hit him with the full force of my seventy-five-pound body.

Barreling down the base path, I could see the fear in Jimmy's eyes. I was confident I had made the right decision. Then came the collision. Jimmy dropped the ball, fell to the ground, and started crying. My plan had worked!

In the midst of my euphoria, as Jimmy lay crying on the ground, and with the sound of my teammates' cheers igniting a huge smile on my face, I touched third base and headed for home. Jimmy was in no condition to throw me out. The catcher waited helplessly at home plate. My mind raced in anticipation of greeting all my buddies as they jumped up and down and screamed with delight.

Approaching glory, just a few strides from the plate, I was jolted from my reverie by the firm and angry hands of a grown man who grabbed me by the shoulders and began screaming at me. The man was Jimmy's father. In my split-second computations between second and third, I had forgotten Jimmy's dad was the home plate umpire. He was angry. Even though my slide into third was just part of playing baseball, I would have to pay for making his boy cry.

Before I had a chance to cross the plate, I was tossed from the game and sent home. Alone. No celebration with my teammates. No pat on the back from our coach.

Silently riding my bike home, I didn't realize I had just experienced something that would serve me for the rest of my life. At the time, all I could think about was getting kicked out of the game. Failure. Making the wrong decision.

For many people, creating a job is first base in the entrepreneurial process. That might look like a journeyman plumber printing his new logo on his truck and branching out on his own; an executive buying a franchise and leaving the safety of the corporate world; or a single parent working the phones while the kids are asleep, trying to drum up multilevel marketing business.

However you get to first base, I honor the courage it takes to just get started. No more paychecks and health insurance. Say goodbye to that company car. Sure, you get to be your own boss, but being on your own is not all sunshine and rainbows. For many of us, there was no choice. We knew this was our path from the beginning.

If things work out, and you survive the start-up phase, you can stay on first forever. Many people do, and there's nothing wrong with that at all. However, if you decide to turn the job you've created into a business, you're headed for second base.

If you have the courage to go for it and find yourself on second base, congratulations. You're in the game!

Be prepared. You may stay on second for a quite a while. In fact, most entrepreneurs never choose to move past this point. And why should they? Owning a retail shop, a restaurant, or a small manufacturing business can provide you with a wonderful life. Perhaps your children can join you in the business and maybe even take it over some day.

Second base can be very safe and financially rewarding. But it revolves around you. Without you, there is no business.

True independence—the freedom most entrepreneurs are seeking—begins to come into focus at third base. This is when your business is running smoothly, providing for all of your family's needs and wants, and possibly providing for many other families as well. You are no longer working in the business. You are working on your legacy.

As with first and second, you can stay on third forever, if you like. For many, there is no reason to leave. They are exactly where they always wanted to be.

Hitting a triple is great. You could, however, go for the home run…

Home plate for an entrepreneur is the complete freedom to live your life as you wish. You may choose to retire and live in paradise, as you define it. You may work on growing your business or buy another one. At home plate, your biggest dreams are now a reality. You made it.

What I thought was failure, as I rode home that day, was really education. The life and fortunes of every entrepreneur are built upon risk. The calculation and management of this risk is what separates us from those who choose to work at a job. We consider the risk/reward ratio, and make our decisions accordingly. Experiencing an error in judgment is part of the entrepreneurial growth process. Experience hones your instincts. And you rely upon your instincts in that nanosecond when a decision must be made.

I failed in my attempt to score, yet I have continued to run the bases. I still get called out every once in a while, but the paralysis of indecision poses a far greater long-term risk to an entrepreneur or an organization than the occasional loss from a calculated risk.

Theodore Roosevelt addressed this very issue in one of his most commonly quoted speeches: "It is not the critic who counts; not the man who points out how the strong man stumbles, or where the doer of deeds could have done them better.

The credit belongs to the man who is actually in the arena, whose face is marred by dust and sweat and blood; who strives valiantly… who at best knows in the end the triumph of high achievement, and who at the worst, if he fails, at least fails while daring greatly."

Is it time for you to get in the arena? I dare you.

# BALANCE VERSUS HARMONY

*I merely took the energy it takes to pout,*
*and wrote some blues.*
—Duke Ellington

GOOGLE "WORK-LIFE BALANCE," AND YOU'LL get over 110,000,000 results. As far as I can tell, none of these results were generated by someone actually able to sustain this perpetually elusive state.

When you think of balance, what comes to mind? Chances are, you visualize an activity or experience with frequent movement and shifting of weight. In sports, for example, skiing and surfing require constant, subtle adjustments in order to stay upright. Golf, often seen as a sport for non-athletes, requires a balanced swing to execute the shots that look so easy on TV. The challenge of riding a bicycle is overcome as we learn to balance our weight on the narrow tires. Even earlier, learning to walk is a formative experience with balance.

As we master walking and riding our bikes, the balance required to avoid sudden and harsh contact with the ground requires little effort. The split-second muscle twitching common to skiers, surfers, and even golfers becomes second nature. We're hardwired for the physical balance required for survival, as we manage our lives subject to the immutable laws of gravity.

In the context of relationships, however, conflict replaces gravity as the challenge to our balance. Consider our legal system: the blindfolded Lady Justice symbolizes the constant need for recalibration in balancing the scales of truth and fairness to arrive at justice. Balance is fleeting, and the act of seeking it implies conflicting interests. Balance is the solution sought to resolve conflict. Absent conflict, what interests would need to be balanced? The need for balance assumes conflict.

Therefore, when balance is our goal, we are, by definition, simultaneously seeking to resolve, thereby staying in conflict. The pursuit of "work-life balance" is guaranteed to be an exercise in frustration and disappointment, fraught with conflict, and keeping us in a perpetual state of conflict management.

This is particularly true for entrepreneurs, who are frequently stuck choosing between family obligations and business demands. Miss the dance recital, and your daughter will be disappointed. Miss a deadline, and you'll lose a huge client and have to lay off staff.

Miss one recital, and she probably won't be scarred for life. Miss recitals, soccer games, and the daddy/daughter dance, and you might pay for it in the form of lingering resentment that will shape decisions for the rest of her life.

The first time you miss a client's deadline, a sincere apology may be accepted. However, the next mistake with that client will probably be your last.

With balance as our goal, we are in a perpetual state of conflict management, forced to choose between competing interests. Relentless scorekeeping by both sides will ensure that there is always at least one aggrieved party, and often both sides will collapse under the weight of the conflict.

I'm not about to propose an easy method for making hard choices. Instead, simply stop striving for balance. In its place, make harmony your target.

In music, harmony is considered to be a pleasing combination of sounds. Relationally, harmony is achieved when various parts of a whole exist in pleasantly coordinated combination with each other. Work-life harmony, then, would result in a business and family with congruent goals designed to work together toward compatible objectives. This is an achievable, sustainable, and collaborative ambition. Interestingly, it is also a state without inherent conflict.

When conflict is introduced to harmony, the result is dissonance. Musically, dissonance is a combination of simultaneously played notes resulting in harsh, unpleasant sounds intended to create tension in the listener. Psychologically, cognitive dissonance is the stress one experiences when holding two conflicting thoughts or values simultaneously.

Countless marriages and families have been torn apart by a dissonant relationship between the entrepreneur's passion for business and her spouse's discomfort with the entrepreneurial life. Having one intention for the business while communicating a conflicting message to your family is a textbook example of cognitive dissonance and a recipe for disaster on at least one, if not both, fronts.

In my experience, the most common source of dissonance between entrepreneur and spouse is a lack of clear communication and understanding. The life of an entrepreneur is difficult enough without having to fight two battles in the trenches; that doesn't sound particularly harmonious. If you think entrepreneurial success is the tonic your family needs to rediscover misplaced joy, happiness, and commitment, you are sorely mistaken. Harmony is what they seek, and you are capable of providing it.

The stress of running a business impacts the entrepreneur and the non-entrepreneurial spouse in different ways. One is making decisions that will have a profound impact on the pair's financial future, while the other is limited to updates from the front.

After a full day spent putting out fires and dodging bullets, when all you want is an hour of decompression before heading back to the office, coming home and being subjected to a thorough debrief is not likely to lead to a relaxing evening.

As entrepreneurs, we tend to be somewhat narcissistic. We have a brilliant idea, come home, and say, "Hi, honey. I quit my job today and bought the donut shop across the street from the plant. The place is always crowded, and we're gonna make a ton of money." Rather than getting high-fives and toasts to our genius, we hear, "Are you kidding me?! What about your 401K? Do you have any idea how many hours a baker works? How could you do this without asking me?"

You can't expect a harmonious response if you blindside your spouse with an unfamiliar or unexpected new tune.

More than one entrepreneur has had to explain sudden loss of income, status, and college funds to a family that counted on her for support. Risk comes with the territory. For an entrepreneur, losing a business or admitting failure may open a deep personal wound. A shattered ego and lost self-esteem are common by-products of the loss.

Unfortunately, I speak from experience on this one. In my mid-thirties, after I'd experienced over ten years of huge financial swings as a commodities and options trader, the market finally dealt me a knockout punch. In the past, I had always managed to get back up, but this one was just too much. I'd been married for less than a year, and, although my wife knew what she was in for when we got married, the swings were taking a toll on her, too.

We had just put down a nonrefundable deposit to buy our first house when I came home shell-shocked and told her I had just lost well over a hundred thousand dollars. That day. She was incredulous.

"How could you lose that much money? I trusted you to be responsible! We just put down a huge deposit on a new house! Now what are we going to do?! I wish you had a job at the post office; at least then I would know where we stood. I could plan, budget. As it is, one day you say we're going to pay cash for this great house, and the next day you come home and tell me you lost almost all of our money. I can't live like this!"

She was right. Losing that much money was a betrayal. I had no business risking our future home. I wasn't thinking of her when I lost the money. Not at all. She didn't even cross my mind until it was too late. In the moment, I let my ego get the best of me. I kept trading bigger and bigger as the day went on, trying to make back the money I'd lost earlier. All I did was lose more. Long before the closing bell, I knew I should stop, but I couldn't. I engineered my own demise. And then I came home and had to tell the woman I loved that I was a failure. Bad day. Very bad day. I'd like some *lifeness*, please.

When the smoke cleared, I realized, *I can't go back to trading. Stacey means more to me than money.* I had to find a way to make a living that honored her aversion to risk, yet still afforded me the opportunity to live passionately.

Balance is really just a juggling act, whereas harmony is bridge-building. The difference is profound. Harmony is the intentional combination of notes or goals for the purpose of creating a pleasing sound or result. Stacey and I were able to build that bridge, and, although the marriage didn't last forever, I believe that the primary reason we've remained friends is the trust we gained in each other from the process of building that bridge.

Once you have agreement, continue to share, ask for help, and allow others to be part of the process. Stacey and I continue to share our feelings as we navigate the parenting process. It's not as if every day is Christmas, but the trust we built during our marriage has carried us through some difficult times. Partnering with the people closest to you makes your dream seem like a collaborative, rather than a solo effort. Significantly, it also gives them the chance to take ownership of the vision and feel like a part of the team. Sharing the vision and engaging all parties in the process: that's a recipe for harmony.

The next time a conflict arises at home or work, try seeking harmony rather than balance. Balance leaves both parties settling for less than they wanted. Harmony allows each one to enjoy the ride. Doesn't harmony feel better than balance?

# IT'S YOUR CALL

*As a start-up CEO, I slept like a baby.*
*I woke up every two hours and cried.*
—Ben Horowitz

CONFESSION: I DON'T HAVE A great job history. I started out with the obligatory paper route—not much fun, but it did provide some spending money. Later, my friend Larry hired me to help him cut the grass at a few homes in the neighborhood—not really much of a résumé builder. In high school, I was a waiter at the local deli until I had a "difference of opinion" with one of the owners. A series of debacles at drug stores, fast-food chains, and travel agencies followed. It was clear that I just wasn't "good employee" material.

My first real break came in Honolulu during my freshman year in college, when I got a job driving a taxi. This was the ideal situation for me. The taxi company charged sixteen dollars per day to rent the cab, and drivers kept all the money they earned. Our cabs were simply regular cars with roof-mounted taxi lights we could take off when we were not working. This solved two problems: I now had a car to get to and from school and I had a job that allowed me to set my own hours. And it didn't hurt that it was a great way to meet tourist girls looking for fun on the island.

I had found a way to make money that didn't involve a boss. This was very cool for a twenty-year-old with a big mouth and authority issues. I learned valuable lessons about time management and got my first taste of entrepreneurship.

I enjoyed being fully responsible for the success or failure of my business. I soon realized that my income was a reflection of the degree to which I committed myself to the work. I could sleep in, go surfing, and work just long enough to pay for food, rent, and cab rental, or work harder and save money. I could wordlessly drive people from place to place or I could tell every tourist in my cab about the island's hidden gems and then offer to take them on a full-day tour at twice the amount I would normally earn in that time.

I have spent the subsequent forty years of my life working for myself in some way or another. As with my trip around the bases, I've experienced some high highs and very low lows. I've used each experience to inform the next step on my journey. Now, I help business owners and entrepreneurs transform their businesses and their lives, giving them the tools they need to succeed. And achieve *lifeness*.

While I still love working for myself, this kind of life is not for everyone.

A couple years after my trading career came to a screeching halt, a group of investors and I purchased the expansion rights to a team in the Continental Basketball Association (CBA). After carefully considering a few other cities in the Midwest, I chose Grand Rapids, Michigan to be the home for my first sports venture, The Grand Rapids HOOPS. The city was clearly on the verge of substantial growth, and had a proud sports tradition. We had a strong following within the community and offered good, clean family entertainment throughout the winter.

As a lifelong Cubs fan, I knew the most important thing we could do was deliver fun to our fans. Wins and losses are tough to control with a tight budget and a league-wide salary cap, but we made sure that smiles were abundant every night. Our halftime entertainment was far more important to most of our fans, for example, than the opposing team or our backup point guard.

Despite a great fan base and a successful team, the local newspaper was relentless in attacking me about everything from press box seating to coaching changes to our cheerleaders' uniforms. The sports editor saw me as an outsider and the wrong person to bring a team to his sports-hungry town. He wasn't about to let the HOOPS's community support and the quality of our product stand in the way of his mission to run me out of town. I had yet to read *The Four Agreements* by Don Miguel Ruiz, so this was long before I'd absorbed the second agreement: Don't take anything personally. At that point in my life, I took *everything* personally.

One night when we were going through a difficult stretch, I listened to a particularly tough road loss on the radio in my office. I went home and couldn't sleep. The paper was winning the battle and breaking me, and, in the process, the team as well. I loved my work, and knew our fans respected our efforts. They saw the work we put into every single aspect of the games and into creating the culture of our franchise. Nonetheless, the constant bombardment of negative energy from the newspaper had become too much for me to bear.

I had thirty investors who trusted me to run the franchise and return a profit, plus ten players, two coaches, and a trainer, all of whom expected major-league perks on a minor-league budget. Advertising, sales, marketing, and PR departments that required state-of-the-art tools to help generate the revenue we needed. And Joannie, our office manager, who controlled the chaos. The stress of keeping everybody satisfied, while doing my best to act as though the pressure wasn't getting to me, had taken its toll.

After that sleepless night, I drove to the office thinking it might be time to throw in the towel. My journey toward harmony had not yet begun, and I had no idea how to find common ground with the newspaper. My mind wandered. Maybe I should sell the team to a local guy, someone the paper could bless as a savior while coasting on the thrill of ridding the town of the Chicago menace. But what if I couldn't find a buyer? How could I go back to my investors and tell them I had failed? I anticipated the shame of telling the members of my staff that their faith in me had been misplaced and that they would have to find new jobs. The agony was overwhelming. I was in full-on victim mode, a pitiful mess. That was my mindset when I pulled into our office parking lot at eight a.m., ready for surrender.

To my surprise, parked at our front door was a shiny new Pontiac Grand Am. That didn't compute. I signed the paychecks, so I knew that no one on our staff was in a position to afford such an extravagance, and it was too early for a salesperson to call.

I had never been able to understand why anyone would choose to just have a job, rather than run his or her own business. Why take orders rather than give them? There was no way I'd allow someone else to control my destiny. Why, I had wondered, would anyone opt for a paycheck rather than a legacy? When I walked into our office, I found my answers.

"Tom, did you see my new car?" Joannie beamed from behind her desk. "Isn't it beautiful? I was so excited that I couldn't wait to get in to show it to you!"

In her excitement, Joannie didn't sense the awkwardness of my response. I felt disoriented, as though a fundamental principle of the universe had just been proven false. I had no idea what to do with this game-changing information. After the requisite pleasantries, I retreated to my office and closed the door.

I sat at my desk, buried my head in my hands, and pondered what I had just learned: I had spent a sleepless night overwhelmed by anxiety about the future of my business and all the lives that would be affected by my failure, while Joannie went out and bought a new car.

She left work, went to a dealership, test-drove a few cars, inhaled the intoxicating new-car smell, spoke with the finance manager, got a loan, traded in her old beater, and drove off the lot with her brand-new car! I went home, wallowed in self-pity, and rolled around in my bed wrapped in a blanket of fear. Who do you think had a better night?

She wouldn't have traded places with me for a million dollars. Why should she? She had an entry-level job that, for her, was easily replaceable. Her needs were modest and could be met just as well at her next job. She lived for her son and her friends and for the rest of her family. If the HOOPS never won another game, her life would remain blissfully carefree.

My ego, my wallet, and my self-esteem were all wrapped up in the team, and failure would not only mean losing my job, but would bring deep shame. All Joannie had to do if the business failed was edit her rèsumè and look for a different place to park her new car from nine to five on weekdays.

Starting your own business can be immensely rewarding and personally gratifying, but there is a potential downside. It can take you away from your friends and family for long stretches of time. You *will* have sleepless nights. Failure is always a looming possibility, and fear is likely to be a frequent companion.

For some, entrepreneurship is not an option. There is no choice to be made. Entrepreneurship chose us. This is who we are at our core. From lemonade stands, Girl Scout cookies, and neighborhood talent shows, we moved on to babysitting, cutting grass, and selling magazine subscriptions door-to-door. By the time we reached adolescence, we knew.

My favorite story about this *knowing* belongs to my friend Angie, who knew she was an entrepreneur before she could spell or define the word. As a child, she picked cherries from the tree in her yard and sold them door-to-door to her neighbors. Other childhood ventures included building an obstacle course in her backyard and charging kids fifteen cents each to test their skills.

Angie left home in her teens, married, and had two kids before turning twenty-one. After a divorce, she struggled to support her family while pursuing her dream to get a degree in social work. Using her long dormant entrepreneurial skills to achieve her goals, she started a shoeshine business inside a country bar. She persuaded the owner to give her the space for a hundred dollars per month, and a friend built a beautiful stand to her specifications. The business soon grew to include stands in several local truck stops. Angie's money and time problems were solved, and she earned that coveted degree and a master's, too! Today, she serves children and families in her thriving practice.

On the other hand, for some, entrepreneurship is best appreciated as a spectator sport.

Joannie wasn't cut out to be an entrepreneur. It wasn't in her nature. But she was completely confident in my ability to guide the HOOPS. She and the rest of my staff slept soundly because they knew I wouldn't let the team fail. They believed in me and my ability to run the business. That was very hard for me to accept during my moment of doubt.

Sometimes the best way to restore your faith in yourself as a leader going through a crisis of confidence is to appreciate your employees' unshakable belief in you. They are singing your song. Look in the mirror and see the powerful, decisive, and principled person to whom they have entrusted their livelihood.

They see your ability to manage risk and to course-correct. They know you're not perfect, but they have no doubt that you're the one they want navigating their ship through troubled waters. You're a leader. That's your job.

# TRUST THE CAIRNS

*Forgiveness is essential to healing,*
*because it requires you to surrender your ego's*
*need to have life fall into place around your*
*personal version of justice.*
—Caroline Myss

WHAT IS A VICTIM? THE definition you'll find in the dictionary will differ a bit from the one I ask you to consider from this point forward.

Merriam-Webster defines a victim as "one that is acted on and usually adversely affected by a force or agent."

*I* define a victim as "one who has abdicated control of his life to powers believed to be beyond his control."

The ironic tyranny of victimhood is that the cruel and oppressive ruler who has condemned you to a life of suffering is... *you*. Living your life as a victim is a matter of choice.

Byron Katie, the author of *Loving What Is: Four Questions That Can Change Your Life*, said, "As long as you think that the cause of your problem is 'out there'—as long as you think that anyone or anything is responsible for your suffering—the situation is hopeless. It means that you are forever in the role of victim."

I repeat. Victimhood is a choice. All victims are volunteers.

I spent large chunks of the first fifty years of my life as a victim. I carried with me all the perceived wrongs I had endured in a metaphorical backpack. I regaled each new person I met with my elaborate tale of woe. I unpacked each offense, and polished it to a radiant shine for all to see.

My mother, father, teachers, landlords, and former bosses were given starring roles in the story of my unfortunate life. By the time I was finished, my audience was in awe of my resilience and convinced I was an extraordinary survivor who miraculously overcame overwhelming odds—or so I thought.

In retrospect, they were probably engulfed by the fumes of my toxic narcissism. I took absolutely no responsibility for any aspect of my life experience, except, of course, my ability to survive in such a hostile environment.

I chose to believe that my problems were due to the actions of others. I felt I had no control over the events in my life. I was the quintessential victim.

Not surprisingly, I was a negativity magnet. Like attracts like. I found harmony in the songs sung by other victims.

So, how did I break out of this death spiral toward martyrdom?

In spite of my propensity for negativity, or perhaps because of it, since early adulthood I had been attracted to self-help books, personal growth seminars, and anything that offered the potential elixir to transform my woe-begotten life. I read *Jonathan Livingston Seagull* and tried EST in the '70s, visited sacred Buddhist shrines in Thailand and read books by Shakti Gawain and Jiddu Krishnamurti in the '80s, and went to weekend "spiritual retreats" and sweat lodges in the '90s while reading *The Alchemist* and *The Artist's Way*.

My life was a perpetual quest for peace and personal happiness. Occasionally, I thought I'd found the answer, but for the most part I simply learned new and different ways to justify my deep-seated belief that life wasn't fair, and I was simply one of the unlucky ones.

By the early 2000s, I'd graduated to staffing events where a new generation of seekers sought to find the missing piece in their lives. At the celebration following one such event, a friend told me about an upcoming weekend retreat in Chicago. I think it was called "Encountering the Beloved." I had no idea what that meant, but it sounded interesting, and I knew I could use more love in my life.

In spite of all the reading and spiritual exploration, I had spent the previous thirty years of my life trying to play the losing hand I had been dealt, with only an occasional glance in the mirror. That was about to change.

Trebbe Johnson was our guide on this weekend forage for spiritual provisions. An experienced storyteller and writer, Trebbe led us on an expedition that, for me, culminated in a conversation with a tree in the middle of a small forest. I wasn't sure what had shifted, but I knew I'd found a teacher whose message resonated in an as-yet-unexplored part of my psyche.

The weekend with Trebbe helped me see that I was not taking responsibility for the circumstances of my life. My perpetual pity party had become a rather lonely celebration, but I had no idea how to change the guest list. That was to be a lesson for another day, but I was getting closer.

John Gardner's words capture the essence of the state from which I needed to escape: "Self-pity is easily the most destructive of the non-pharmaceutical narcotics; it is addictive, gives momentary pleasure, and separates the victim from reality."

As my weekend drew to a close, I approached Trebbe and inquired about other events she had on her calendar. She mentioned that she would be co-guiding a vision quest in southeastern Utah in about six months. I signed up on the spot, in spite of the fact that I had absolutely no idea what a vision quest was.

I soon learned that a vision quest was a rite of passage, historically practiced in many Native American cultures by young males transitioning from adolescence into adulthood. More recently, wilderness schools have introduced the practice to non-Native groups of both men and women.

My fellow questers and I would be spending ten days in the wilderness. During that time, we would fast for four days, the last three of which would be spent alone, far from our base camp and each other. I had grown up in the suburbs, where watching a squirrel run up a tree qualified as a wildlife experience. This was way out of my comfort zone.

Trebbe gave me a list of supplies to bring, which included a sleeping bag, tarp, knife, and some rope. No tent. I was so naïve and eager to continue the journey that began with my conversation with a tree in Chicago that I had no fear at all. That came later.

Over the next few weeks, I began to work on my intention for the quest. What did I want to accomplish in the wilderness? I knew this was more than a physical challenge and I wanted to go as deep into myself as possible. The intention I came up with was to release all the victim energy I'd been carrying around for as long as I could remember.

The ensuing months before leaving for Utah were spent exploring the barriers that stood between me and liberation from a lifetime of victimhood. My savant-like ability to remember every person who had ever done me wrong, coupled with a resolute determination to take each event personally, left me with a seemingly limitless list of injustices to buttress my claim that my life really sucked. Absent a formal apology from my tormentor that included complete absolution for any contribution I made to the situation, there was virtually no way I could move past any grievance.

Got forgiveness? Not so much.

With help from my very patient therapist, Justine, I began the process of letting go. First, I had to redefine forgiveness. For me, the act of forgiveness was to pardon, condone, forget, or pretend the wounding behavior or act had never even happened. I saw forgiveness as minimizing the perceived wrong. No way! I couldn't do that. I wanted justice before I would grant forgiveness!

Wow. That definition was guaranteed to keep me perpetually stuck. Clearly, learning to forgive wasn't going to happen overnight. However, as I became willing to entertain a different definition, I began to see forgiveness as an evolution, a process.

The *New World Encyclopedia* defines forgiveness as "the mental, emotional, and spiritual process of letting go of resentment, indignation, or anger toward another person for a perceived offense, difference, or mistake. It can also mean ceasing to demand punishment or restitution for transgressions real or imagined."

For most people, forgiveness is an acquired taste—initially, overwhelmingly bitter. Over time, and with Justine's help, the new outlook of forgiveness as a process allowed me to entertain the possibility that I could leave the life of a victim behind.

Additionally, Justine had given me another assignment. She suggested that I expand my stated intention. My full intention became, *I will release all the victim energy inside me and replace it with the love that was there in the first place.* Whoa! That took this quest to a whole new level. Now I not only had to forgive the people and circumstances that had conspired to hurt me, but I also had to fill the new vacancy in my heart with love. That's extreme vulnerability. I was entering uncharted territory.

I arrived in Utah a few days before the rest of the group, still carrying my bag of injustices in search of appropriate retribution. In spite of all the preparatory work I had done, I had no idea how I would let them go. In fact, I doubted that I would.

I spent my pre-quest days hiking the stunning slickrock trails and canyons around Moab. In late July, most of the locals wisely leave town or stay inside most of the day. The heat was intense, and most guidebooks suggest avoiding Utah in July and August, so I had many of the trails to myself.

This turned out to be a perfect way to begin the forgiveness process. Characteristically, I had done very little preparation for the physical part of my journey. My lingering adolescent assumptions of personal indestructability added an element of danger to the already challenging hikes. As my body struggled to adjust to the extreme climate and unfamiliar physical challenges, I had to trust the rock piles—called cairns—that marked the trails to keep me safe and on course. For an inexperienced hiker with a very poor sense of direction, asthma, and an outsized fear of wild animals—both dead and alive—this was a tall order.

The first crack in the armor protecting my heart came at the end of my second hike, as I spotted the trailhead after about half an hour of overheated uncertainty. The cairns on the trail had seemed to indicate that I wasn't lost, but nothing looked familiar. I had been scared and didn't have the supplies to last long in the oppressive heat.

When I realized I was safe, I suddenly began to cry. I cried as I thought of all the love that had gone into supporting me that day. I'd hiked without a compass or a map—brilliant, I know—and followed trail markers left by anonymous guides. Others who had hiked the trail before me had left the cairns intact and in place. No animals, careless visitors, or weather events had disturbed the markers. Any break in that chain could have been disastrous. I was overwhelmed with gratitude.

Gratitude. An unexpected but essential step in the forgiveness process. With no one at hand to thank, I was overcome with emotion. Gratitude is a positive response to good things that happen to us. It comes with the acknowledgment that the source of that goodness is outside of us. I chose to feel gratitude. In that moment, the choice was spontaneous.

Forgiveness is also a choice. I wasn't there yet, but the seeds were being planted for me to realize that I could choose to forgive as easily as I could choose to feel grateful. Unquestionably, there was pain and hurt in my past. But, I was getting closer to a place from which I could choose to let the pain continue to hurt me or simply let it go. I could release it and create a new story. An empowering story. My story.

To create this new story, I had to take another giant step. To cross over from victim to victor, I had to take responsibility for the circumstances in my life. Uncompromising responsibility. For everything.

In his book *Man's Search for Meaning,* Victor Frankl found the power to survive the Nazi death camps in Auschwitz, Poland by realizing that "to choose one's attitude in any given set of circumstances, is to choose one's own way in life. Everything can be taken from a man but …the last of the human freedoms—to choose one's attitude in any given set of circumstances."

My life story certainly doesn't include anything remotely comparable to the unspeakable horror of being confined in a concentration camp. Frankl's choice was far more heroic than mine. His lesson, however, is universal.

Whatever the story, we do not have to keep repeating it. We can create a new story. A powerful story. The story of a victor, not a victim.

We have the power to choose. We can choose to forgive or we can choose to hold on to our grievances and perpetually use them to slay our tormentors. Forgiveness is not something we bestow upon a remorseful adversary. It is a gift we give ourselves. And it is a gift that will keep on giving, as it vanquishes the victim we have become.

# ROCKS? WHAT ROCKS?

*The biggest obstacle to taking a bigger
perspective on life is that our emotions
capture and blind us.*
—Pema Chödrön

BEFORE LEAVING MOAB TO BEGIN the vision quest, Trebbe,
her co-guide, Louden Kiracofe, and five other brave souls
like me, performed a ceremony on the banks of the Colorado
River to honor our upcoming pilgrimage and embrace the
unknown experiences that would define our quests. As we
crossed the threshold to begin our individual journeys, we
interrupted the "time" of our everyday lives to enter "Sacred
Time," in which each moment contains a grain of divine
opportunity. In ten days, we would return to the river and

cross the threshold back to the world we left behind. Until then, Sacred Time. Harmonic Time.

Our ages ranged from twenty to nearly seventy, and we had come from various parts of the country to join together for what was a deeply personal, individual journey. With fear, excitement, and eager anticipation, we began the drive to base camp. We were our own little community now, and each of us hoped to return to the communities we had left behind changed in some way.

My twin goals, of releasing the burden of the victim energy that had defined me for so long and replacing it with the love that was there in the first place, were still a stretch. But they were beginning to feel possible.

Over the next three days, Trebbe and Louden introduced us to the natural beauty surrounding our campsite and taught us skills we would need to stay safe in the wilderness. For a city boy like me, this included basics like tying a slipknot, staying hydrated, and using natural landmarks to keep from getting lost.

Early on our fourth morning, we set out on our solo time in the wilderness. We had begun our fast the day before and would be alone with our thoughts for the next three full days. We had no food, but ample water. No tent, but a sleeping bag, tarp, and some rope. No books or phones, but paper and a journal. We were alone.

I was petrified. Sleeping outside was bad enough when I was surrounded by other people who seemed to be at ease with outdoor living, but being alone in the silent darkness filled me with horror. I felt totally vulnerable. Visions of lions and tigers and bears were occasionally interrupted by panic at the thought of unknown vermin crawling all over my sleeping, defenseless body.

Somehow, I made it through the night. I actually slept pretty well.

The precise moment when I realized I had accomplished my goal was unexpectedly quiet. I had expected—if it were to happen at all—some profound epiphany, punctuated by a thunderclap of acknowledgment from the Universe, something like, *"YOUR LIFE HAS CHANGED. IT IS NOW SAFE TO GO BACK IN THE WATER."* Well, not exactly.

I crawled out of my sleeping bag and inhaled the early morning breath of the canyon. I stood on a rock ledge and saw nothing but beauty spread out before me. I began to say a prayer of gratitude for making it through the night when I realized it was gone. My bag of rocks was gone. No epiphany. No lightning or thunder. Just gone.

My gratitude for the cairns opened the space for me to see the beauty that surrounded me. The darkness of my self-imposed victimhood was overcome by the light I chose to see.

Gratitude opened the door to forgiveness. With forgiveness came the power to finally leave the self-pity behind. Victims are powerless. I now had the power to overcome the most significant obstacle to my own success: me.

My years of refusing to forgive others had thwarted any opportunity for me to be a leader. No one follows a victim. Victims don't inspire followers. I had always wanted to be a leader and I was now able to begin to build my platform.

Lest you think that going from victim to victor is as simple as fasting for a few days in the wilderness, I have some bad news for you. It is an ongoing challenge. You will struggle and fall. Just when you think you're ready to chill with the Dalai Lama, some guy with a cowboy hat will sit in front of you at the movie theater and loudly tell his friend how the movie ends before the opening credits finish rolling. Of course, as the self-appointed caretaker of the universe, you will decide to take it upon yourself to teach him a lesson in movie theater etiquette. After you and the offender exchange blows and are escorted out of the theater, the rest of the audience will erupt in spontaneous applause. The road to enlightenment is not a smooth ride.

Over the years, some of my attempts to maintain harmony have ended better than others. That's what life looks like. We're all works in progress, with the power to choose our response to every event in our lives. Let's do our best to choose wisely. And don't start a fight at *The Muppet Movie*. You're better than that.

# FOUL BALLS AND LIMITING BELIEFS

*If you always put limits into everything you do,*
*physical or anything else, it will spread into*
*your work and into your life. There are no*
*limits, there are only plateaus, and you must*
*not stay there, you must go beyond them.*
—Bruce Lee

I GREW UP JUST OUTSIDE Chicago in a very polarized neighborhood. You were either a Cubs fan or a White Sox fan. There was no middle ground and absolutely no flip-flopping based on how the teams were doing. Of course, if winning had been the standard, there would have been no Cubs fans, but that's another story. My father was a Cubs fan, so I became a Cubs fan. It was as simple as that. Anyway, by the time I was eleven or twelve, my parents allowed me to go to Cubs games with friends. Just us kids. No parents. Since the Cubs played only day games at Wrigley Field back then, we could leave around lunchtime and be home before dinner.

At that age, we all brought our mitts to the game, since we hoped to catch any foul ball or home run that came our way. The likelihood of catching a ball may have been remote, but we were there, gloves at the ready, just in case.

My father, professional pessimist that he was, would generally try to dissuade me from bringing my mitt for all sorts of adult reasons that made no sense to me:

One: I might lose it. Well, that was ridiculous, because it would be on my left hand the whole time, except, of course, when I was shoving hot dogs, peanuts, or Cracker Jack into my mouth. At those times, I would be sitting on it. Losing my glove wasn't an option.

Two: It might get stolen by some big kids aiming to start trouble. My father's inherent paranoia was on display here. Thuggery at Wrigley Field in the early sixties? About as likely as the Cubs winning the World Series.

Three: His final point was always the math. He would tell me that even if there were only three thousand people in attendance, my chances of catching a ball were remote. At this point he usually reminded me of the probability that we'd get kicked out of the box seats when the ushers realized our tickets were for the left field bleachers.

My father's words had absolutely zero impact on my decision. I brought my mitt.

So, on this particular day, Lee and I went to the game, mitts in hand, to cheer on our beloved Cubs. I was with my best friend in the world, free from the past, with no thought of the future. We were living perfectly in the moment. Catching a ball wouldn't make or break the day. The most important thing, always, was a Cubs victory. I can't tell you how many nights I cried myself to sleep over a Cubs loss, but that never dulled my enthusiasm for the next game.

When you're twelve and go to a game without adults, you get to the game early. Very early. As soon as the gates open. Lee and I would watch batting practice, bug players for autographs, sneak down into the box seats (and hope the real owners of the seats wouldn't show up), and spend all of our food money before the game even started. On this day, we expected nothing different.

Our first big break came during batting practice. This may not count as catching a ball, but, shortly after we arrived, I saw a ball bouncing down the steps of the aisle as we were walking to our seats. It must have been a batting-practice foul ball. We didn't see it hit. There were just a few people in the stands and no one was running to get it, so I just picked it up. My first Major League ball. I couldn't wait to get home and tell my father how I leaped high over the head of some six-foot tall gang member to snare a home run ball off the bat of my hero, Ernie Banks.

The excitement of holding an actual Major League ball was overwhelming. Once the game started, people asked me about it, and I repeated the somewhat lame story of the bouncing ball from nowhere. Nonetheless, I was still beaming over my new treasure.

Another thing that kids do when they go to games without their parents is stay until the game is over, regardless of the score or the weather. In the ninth inning of another blowout loss, Lee and I were among the few fans left. A foul ball was hit high into the air behind the Cubs' dugout, which happened to be the general area where we were sitting. We both jumped from our seats in pursuit of glory.

Catching a foul ball at a Major League game involves a few variables. When there are tons of people at the game, the ball practically has to land in your lap, so you are limited in terms of geography. A virtually empty stadium presents different issues. Maneuvering around the seats and railings without hitting something hard is essential. Doing all this while keeping your eye on the ball takes real skill. On this day, I had the skill.

As the ball came down, I was in prime position to make the play, but a scrum of five or six other kids had the same idea. I jumped as high as I could, with one unwavering intention: Make The Catch. When the ball landed in my glove, I felt a euphoria unequaled by any other experience in my young life. I landed in a heap on the concrete steps with a couple kids on top of me, but I held on tight and emerged triumphant with my prize. I floated back to my seat, my cheeks flushed with pride, to the sound of "Nice catch, kid," from a couple of men finishing off their last beers. That was one of the best days of my childhood.

Of course, the sacred spheres I brought home that day didn't stop my father from continuing to tell me to leave the mitt at home. But this proved to be an early lesson in not allowing the limiting beliefs and negative energy of others to poison my well of joy and hope. My father's contentions were reasonable, and his math was probably right, but I knew something that he didn't. I knew that I was open to the possibility that I could get what I wanted, that I could reach my goals. This is a lesson I've had to relearn a few times over the years, when I've allowed my own limiting beliefs to sabotage my dreams.

Well-meaning "voices of reason" can trample the passion of a vulnerable entrepreneur. Differentiating between good advice and someone else's (or your own) limiting beliefs can be a formidable challenge. My advice: Bring your mitt.

# PRIZE? WHAT PRIZE?

*I've trained all my life not to be*
*distracted by distractions.*
—Nik Wallenda

"KEEP YOUR EYES ON THE prize" is an overused catchphrase that is supposed to remind us to pay attention to our ultimate goal even while we temporarily focus on the task at hand. The problem for many entrepreneurs is that we can be easily distracted by the urgency in front of us, and lose sight of the "prize" upon which we set the course for our journey. Sometimes, we allow our urgent distraction to become the new "prize." Sound familiar?

In business, while our senses are acutely tuned to the input we receive from clients and customers, employees and management—even our own intuition—our success is dependent upon our ability to stay in alignment with our fundamental mission. We may recalibrate our compass in response to changing market conditions and new information, but our purpose needs to remain in perpetual focus.

Frequently, this is easier said than done.

The Grand Rapids HOOPS were not as well funded as most of the other teams in the CBA, and, in order to survive, we had to actually *make* money—a novel idea in Minor League sports at that time. To ensure our success on the court as well as at the box office, I was determined to learn from the mistakes made by wealthier teams.

I believed that, for us to be successful, we needed to create a "sellout mentality" in the community. If tickets were abundantly available, they would have little perceived value, and there would be no compelling reason for anyone to buy tickets before the night of the game. With no motivation for advance purchase, a sudden snowstorm could deliver a devastating blow to our bottom line. Therefore, our success was directly tied to creating ticket value.

I chose to play in the smallest arena in the league, rather than in one where "ticket giveaways" would be the only way to fill the place. Our thirty-two-hundred-seat building was perfect. The sight lines were excellent, parking was convenient, and seats were in limited supply.

The first task for the sales staff was to sell as many season tickets as possible. My goal was to have half the arena sold to season ticket holders before we put any single game tickets on sale. Mission accomplished.

Next, we focused on selling out opening night. For three months, my mantra was, "Opening night *must* be a sellout." Everyone on our staff bought into this mission, and plans for opening night dominated our thoughts and conversations.

Roughly a week before opening night, we had reached our goal. We were excited and proud.

The league commissioner attended the game and was visibly impressed. He noted that this was the first time in his career that he had seen ticket scalpers in front of a CBA arena.

With the game underway and the excitement palpable, I decided to drop by the box office to ask a question that had not even crossed my mind before that moment: "How are we looking for game two, on Tuesday?"

Hard to believe, but I had been so wrapped up in season ticket sales, corporate sponsorships, opening night, and in establishing our sellout bona fides that I had completely lost sight of the rest of the story: We had an entire season ahead of us.

The news from the box office slapped the opening-night smile off my face before the end of the first quarter! We had sold fewer than a hundred single game tickets for game two.

I was astounded by my own stupidity. How could I have overlooked something so obvious? What would people say when they showed up for the next game and saw a half-empty arena? Would our season ticket holders want their money back? Would they conclude that the first night was a fluke? Well, the naysayers did have a field day, but their joy didn't last long.

Our second game drew the smallest crowd in the five years of my stewardship.

We refused to let that hiccup define us, so we immediately implemented a strategy focused on each of the remaining home games. We marketed our halftime entertainment to children and families. We put together weeknight packages and special nights for businesses and schools. We enlisted the support of our corporate sponsors, who had a vested interest in our success.

The new strategy worked. Over the course of the season, we sold over eighty percent of our tickets, and most weekend games were sold out or close to it.

Fortunately, we managed to survive my hyper-focus on an opening night sellout. The true measure of our success was driven by sustained attendance and corporate support. I had known that all along, but I lost sight of it by narrowly focusing on just one component of the big picture.

Simply keeping my eyes on the prize wasn't enough for me. I needed a further reminder. Perhaps this cross pollination of tired idioms will help keep the entrepreneur in you from falling victim to defeat by distraction: Don't change prizes in the middle of the stream.

# MONEY, VALUE, AND PB&J

*Nowadays, people know the price of*
*everything and the value of nothing.*
—Oscar Wilde

IN MY LATE TWENTIES, I suffered a significant business setback. After riding pretty high and living the fantasy life of a young trader with no responsibilities or concern for the future, I made a series of very poor decisions that left me embarrassed and nearly broke. Faced with the reality of my bleak financial situation, I realized I had been consumed by the business and hadn't stopped for even a moment to truly appreciate the monetary success I was having.

I started making good money right out of college and never checked the price of anything. If I wanted something and had the money in my pocket, I bought it. I once walked into a car dealership, saw a car I liked, and wrote a check for the amount on the sticker. I had no idea you were supposed to negotiate! The salesman must have started laughing the moment I walked out the door. I bought a motorcycle in exactly the same way. I knew I was fortunate to be able to buy these things, but since the money was coming in so easily, the value I placed on the purchases was insignificant.

Unfortunately, before the newness had worn off, I had to drive back to the same car dealership and then walk home with a much smaller check than the one I'd written earlier. When I tried to sell the motorcycle, they offered me so little I figured I'd keep it and save on cab fares. A week later it was stolen. Uninsured.

I decided to step away from trading completely and travel. I had no idea how long I'd be gone, but I simply shut down the business and left town. I didn't have too much money left and had no idea if I'd ever be able to make back what I'd lost, but I knew I needed a more respectful relationship with money.

My clearest intention for the journey was to learn the value of a dollar and develop the discipline to make reasoned spending and saving choices.

During nearly a year of living out of my backpack, I hiked stunning trails in New Zealand, experienced the desolation of the Australian Outback, cheated death in Thailand, taught English in Japan, and had ample time for self-reflection. Throughout my travels, I never lost sight of my intention.

Lake Toba is a large natural lake on the island of Sumatra in western Indonesia. In the middle of that lake is a little island with a few shacks among the vegetation. The total cost for my room and food for one week in this remote tropical paradise was seven dollars. One day, as I took a walk around the island, I came upon a little shop. It sold a bit of everything: clothes, medicine, food, and the one taste I missed more than any other, peanut butter. Creamy Skippy. Not my favorite brand, but the moment I saw it, I was overcome with longing.

I took it down from the shelf and smiled at the simple joy of holding the jar. I opened it and inhaled the intoxicating smell I had missed for so long. I thought of my peanut butter history: on white bread with grape jelly after school, sometimes with potato chips between the slices; on rye toast with strawberry jam and an additional layer of real butter. I thought about finding bread and jelly to complete the feast. Maybe I could even find a toaster!

Before searching further, I checked the price: five dollars. Five dollars for a very small jar of creamy Skippy. This was almost as much as I was paying for an entire week on the island! Add the cost of bread and jelly, and I could be looking at tripling my island expenditures. My intention was to learn the value of a dollar, and I'd walked right into a perfect opportunity to observe my behavior and see how far I'd come.

I doubt anyone in the store was aware of my dilemma, but I had quite an active conversation with myself. Before the trip, I'd made and lost thousands of dollars in a matter of minutes during the course of an average day. Back then, five dollars couldn't have been less significant. Now I was paying seven dollars in exchange for an entire week of food and shelter on this little slice of heaven. It just didn't make sense to triple that for a few moments of sugary bliss.

The knowledge that, by delaying my gratification, I would be taking a huge step toward the positive change I was seeking made closing the jar and returning it to the shelf only slightly easier. I knew it was the best choice, but I sure wanted my PB&J.

Later that evening, I ran into fellow American reading a copy of the *Wall Street Journal* that he had purchased a few days earlier in Singapore. I was interested in catching up on the news, but I was distracted by his strange headset that was attached to a metal thing about the size of a paperback book.

When he finished reading, he handed me the newspaper, took off his headset, and introduced himself. Rather abruptly, I asked him about the metal thing. He passed me the headset and motioned for me to put it on. I was astounded to hear Earth, Wind, and Fire coming through loud and clear.

What was this thing, and where could I get one? Even more than I missed peanut butter, I missed easy access to music while I was traveling, and this could be the perfect solution. That, my friends, was my introduction to the Sony Walkman.

When I'd left home about seven months earlier, no such thing existed. Now I couldn't live without it. My new friend told me that the Walkman was available in Singapore, the next stop on my journey, for about a hundred bucks.

A couple days later, after a long wait to get through customs and a quick trip to drop off my backpack at my hotel, I headed straight for the commercial district to purchase a Walkman and to revisit the PB&J lesson, this time with startlingly different results.

In search of my prize, I walked into the first electronics store I saw. The polite sales clerk explained with a shrug that they were completely sold out of the Walkman, notwithstanding the box I could clearly see in the window display. Strange, but… okay. The same thing happened at the next store. And the next. And the next.

Frustrated and angry, I didn't understand what was happening. All these stores clearly had the product, but were unwilling to sell it to me. Why? Was it because I was American? Was I violating some unknown protocol?

I'm a determined guy and I wasn't leaving Singapore without a Walkman, so, when my request was greeted with the same forlorn response at the next store, I said, "I understand that you are currently out of the Walkman, but, if you did have one, what would it cost?"

"One hundred dollars."

"Okay, if I had a hundred and twenty-five dollars, do you think you could find one for me?"

"No, sir."

"One-fifty?"

"I'm sorry sir, we are sold out," the clerk replied.

"One-seventy-five?"

"I wish I could help you, sir, but we don't have one to sell."

"Wow. That's too bad, because I sure would like a Walkman," I said. "I'd never seen one until a couple days ago and now I don't think I can live without the sound of music in my ears while I'm traveling. How about two hundred dollars? Do you think if I had two hundred dollars I could get a Walkman?" At this point, I pulled out two one hundred-dollar bills.

"Let me go in the back and check for you."

Within moments, she reappeared with a brand-new, shrink-wrapped Walkman in her hands. "Here you go, sir. That will be two hundred dollars, please."

I left with my Walkman, and she earned an extra hundred bucks. Seemed like a fair exchange to me.

Less than forty-eight hours earlier, I had been unwilling to spend five dollars for a jar of my favorite food—a taste I had craved for months. I couldn't justify it based upon the value of a dollar in a remote part of Indonesia.

Now, I was happy to pay two hundred dollars—double the list price—for a device that would allow me to hear familiar music while I was in a foreign land.

My intention had been tested. How did I do?

On the island, where the charge for a week of room and board was seven dollars, putting the peanut butter back on the shelf made perfect sense. I didn't need the food, and eating the sandwich would not have brought me joy commensurate with the relative increase in cost of the week.

In Singapore, however, where my hotel room cost a hundred dollars per night, spending two hundred dollars to hear music for the next five months was an easy decision to make. The value was clearly present. Two hundred dollars in exchange for months of musical enjoyment trumps five dollars for an hour of frivolous indulgence any day.

The rest of my trip was great, and I learned far more about comparative value than I had envisioned before I left. This lesson in particular has stayed with me ever since, serving me well throughout my entrepreneurial career.

There are times when money is flowing, and expansion can be easily financed out of current revenues, yet six months later you may need to take out a high-interest loan to cover payroll. One moment you're working out of your basement, and the next you pick up a new customer and suddenly need a five thousand-square-foot warehouse with a loading dock.

Effective decisions are made in the context of current conditions and the best available prognostications for the future. Assuming the value of a product or service will remain static regardless of prevailing factors and conditions is to court disaster.

By the way, if we find ourselves stranded on a deserted island with limited provisions, you can have the Walkman while I ration the Skippy.

# THE BEST THANKSGIVING EVER

*When we set expectations around specific
outcomes, we limit what is possible.*
—Roger Nix

I KEEP A RUNNING LIST of things I would like to do, to be,
to accomplish, to learn, etcetera, in the calendar on my desk.
Periodically, I'll sit back and review it. Some things have been
on the list for years and others fall off as my interests change.
For some, their time simply hasn't come yet. Other things,
however, just seem to happen, almost without effort, merely
by virtue of sending the message to the universe that I am
open to the possibility.

I've noticed that some goals, which once seemed so out
of reach and have been long since forgotten, have a way of
coming to pass, seemingly on their own. It's as though simply

setting the intention and then letting go of my expectations has given them the room to grow and actualize.

Checking the list will occasionally remind me of something I'd like to do, and at that moment I am suddenly ready to put a plan into action to accomplish it. For example, a few years ago, one desire that had been on my list for quite some time was to see Leonard Cohen in concert.

I remember writing it down one day after hearing a cut from his *Live in London* album. It was something I knew I wanted to get around to, and, since the award-winning songwriter was in his mid-seventies, there was some sense of urgency in my intention.

Time passed, and one early spring day I googled Leonard Cohen to see if he had a tour coming up. Sure enough, he was scheduled to be in Chicago the day after Thanksgiving. I impulsively bought two tickets for the show.

As a displaced Chicagoan living in Dayton, Ohio, I figured the concert would be a great start to a romantic weekend getaway. I could show off my hometown, visit old friends, and hear some great music. I'd been divorced for over ten years, wasn't dating anyone at the time, and had absolutely no prospects, so the purchase presented a bit of a personal challenge, a way to help me reach another one of my goals: being in a loving, lasting, "finally forever" kind of relationship.

The tickets arrived, I put them up on my bulletin board where I could see them every day, and I did my best to manifest the woman of my dreams. I liked the way I was using the energy of realizing one goal to propel me toward another. It seemed so perfectly synergistic.

Spring turned into summer, which made way for another beautiful autumn, and, although there were a couple false alarms, "she" had yet to appear. The tickets stayed front and center, and my "trust in the process" began to wear a bit thin. Would I be sitting next to an empty seat? What was wrong with me?

As the date of the concert drew near, I was still dateless. Looking for a backup plan, I called friends in Chicago to see if anyone would be interested in joining me, just in case "she" did not appear. With every "Sorry, I already have plans," I heard another door slam on my "synergistic" manifestation. Even my sister had better things to do. Ouch!

About a week before the concert, Sam asked me if I was busy the day after Thanksgiving. There was no school that Friday, and he wanted to hang out.

I started to tell him that I was going to Chicago for a concert, but my heart just wouldn't let me do it. I had spent a lot of money on the tickets and nine months or so pining for "the woman" who would walk into my life and join me for this romantic weekend. Sam was not the date I had in mind, but when my favorite human being in the whole wide world asked if we could just hang out, I couldn't say no.

So there he was, my romantic date: Sam Rubens.

In typical Sam fashion, as soon as we got in the car and before we even got on the highway to Chicago, he said, "Daddy, thank you so much for taking me with you to see Leonard Cohen. I am having so much fun. Can we do this again sometime?"

You can probably guess the rest. We had a great time, stayed in a suite at a nice hotel, talked and listened to music on the ride back and forth from Dayton, and cemented a memory that would stay with us forever. Sounds pretty romantic to me!

Plans are essential to moving toward our dreams and goals, and setting an intention serves as a positive reminder of what we want to accomplish. The burden of expectation, however, can be the enemy of the best intentions.

Had I been inflexible and unable to accept any alteration of my expectation of a romantic weekend with a new sweetheart, I probably would have stayed home and let the tickets go to waste. Fortunately, I stayed open to the possibility that a different type of romance might appear.

Are your intentions being undermined by unwavering expectations?

I had assumed that the romantic getaway I sought would involve an as-yet-unmet woman. The universe had another idea. Not surprisingly, the universe was right. And that, my friends, is the story of my best Thanksgiving. Ever.

# RAVING FAN OR LOST CUSTOMER—YOU MAKE THE CHOICE

*The weak can never forgive.*
*Forgiveness is the attitude of the strong.*
—Gandhi

I DON'T SUBSCRIBE TO THE theory that the customer is always right, but treating them with respect is non-negotiable. If you sell a product or provide a service, your mission statement probably includes a reference to customer service and satisfaction.

For example, Nordstrom's mission is to "offer the customer the best service, selection, quality and value."

"I'm sorry you're disappointed with our service," expresses regret for the result, not the precipitating action. The subtle shift to, "I'm sorry our service didn't meet your expectations," acknowledges your responsibility to serve your customer and your failure to do so on this occasion. Harmony in action.

According to Merriam-Webster, an apology is an "expression of regret for having done or said something wrong."

Making a mistake, disappointing a customer, and even delivering poor service can be a great business growth tool. It provides you the opportunity to offer a sincere apology and make amends for your mistake. By immediately seeking harmony rather than making an excuse, you have a customer who knows she will be treated fairly, in good times and bad.

This strategy works particularly well with your loudest critics. In the first season for the Grand Rapids HOOPS, we were the subject of quite a few letters to the editor printed in the local paper. Many were positive, but some were not, and the negative comments hurt me. I took great pride in our product and felt it deeply when we were not received well. Our mission was "to bring good, clean, family entertainment to our community." When we failed, fixing the problem was imperative.

One particularly negative letter inspired me to take action. The writer was unhappy with the halftime entertainment at a particular game. While I couldn't control wins and losses, I was fully responsible for every other part of the fan experience.

The event that upset her was bear wrestling. At halftime during a recent game, a bear was brought out to center court, and courageous fans were invited to come down to wrestle him. The letter writer felt it was degrading to the animal and inappropriate for families. Her comments were harsh, and she mentioned me by name.

She signed the letter, so I found her phone number and gave her a call. You can imagine her surprise when she picked up the phone and heard, "Hello Mary, this is Tom Rubens from the HOOPS, how are you today?"

The silence was profound. I pictured her looking at the phone, wondering which one of her friends was setting her up. Her uncertain reply was, "I'm fine."

"Mary, I'm calling in response to the letter from you that appeared in the paper today and I owe you an apology." More silence.

"Halftime entertainment is my responsibility, and I do my best to bring in acts that our fans will enjoy. Last night, I failed you and I am very sorry."

"Really?" By the tone of her voice, I could tell she still thought this might be a joke.

"Yes. When I hired the act, I thought it would be fun to see ordinary people get into the ring with a bear. It would terrify me, and I looked forward to watching others take the challenge. Your letter, as well as comments from other fans, helped me see the event differently. I was wrong. My idea of fun required the probable drugging and mistreatment of the bear. I am so sorry for that and feel terrible now that I realize what I have done. I hope you'll forgive me and give The HOOPS another chance to earn your trust."

"Wow. Mr. Rubens, I never expected you to care about my opinion and I certainly didn't expect this call. Thank you so much."

Then came the real shift. "I'm sorry for the harsh tone of my letter. I was angry and sent it without considering your perspective. The games are so much fun! We love the music, the mascot, and the way your players interact with fans after the game. My husband and I were so happy when we read about the team coming to town, and your call today reminds me of the excitement we felt when we heard the news."

She responded to my effort to harmonize with her own harmonization. Perfect! The rest of the call was just what you'd expect. An unhappy customer became a fan for life. I invited her and her husband to be my guests at the next game, and she told her friends that the owner of the team called her to apologize about the bear.

Our mission was deeply imbedded in our culture. When we failed, apologizing and doing our best to make it right was the only alternative.

The difference between a raving fan and a lost customer can be as small as a few well-chosen words and responsible accountability. Mastering the art of sincere apology will serve you well in all your relationships. You honor the recipient by acknowledging responsibility, and your subsequent actions illustrate your commitment to harmony and accountability. Harmony. Accountability. What a great way to cement a friendship and secure a lifelong customer.

## 12

# HARMONY IS ELUSIVE

*I've heard it said that Bach questioned whether the soloist or the accompanist deserves the greater glory.*
—Nancy Moser

FREQUENTLY, ENTREPRENEURS HAVE A DIFFICULT time with harmony. We tend to be cowboys or cowgirls who are used to making all the big decisions. We may not even understand the question, but we're ready with a strong answer. Harmony can get in the way when we're moving full steam ahead toward a goal, particularly when we haven't shared that goal with anyone else.

According to my friend and fellow business coach, Dave Dudon, "It's not in the nature of the entrepreneur to lead a harmonious life. I work to mitigate, rather than solve, the problem."

I'm a bit more optimistic about it than Dave, but I understand his point. I fully agree with him when he says that "driven, creative entrepreneurs frequently fall in love with, and are married to, their business. Many CEOs are on their second marriages because their relentless quest for success, if not shared by their spouse, will often feel like a betrayal."

Here's how Dave keeps harmony at the forefront. "For this reason, I ask my clients to give my phone number to their spouse, who is free to call me at any time. I refer to spouses as the 'trust officers' for the business. I say that because they make sure the CEO honors the best interests of the business without neglecting the family commitments he or she has made. This leads to a feeling of collaboration, rather than betrayal."

I love that!

Early in his engagement, Dave lets his clients paint the visions of their companies. When these pictures become clear, he then asks clients to share them with the ones they love. When spouses and family members are on board with the visions, they are far more likely help the CEOs stay focused on what is truly important. *Lifeness*!

I've had the chance to watch Dave work, and he integrates home and family into his annual reviews and quarterly tune-ups. Each meeting begins with everyone present sharing good news, both personal and professional. Key stakeholders set personal and professional goals that are reviewed quarterly. These reviews reinforce the importance of each goal in the achievement of success. They also encourage harmony within the organization and allow business associates to become accountability partners, helping each other keep commitments to both business and family.

Dave's point is that harmony is an elusive target for the hyper-focused entrepreneur. I heartily agree, although it is important to recognize that a recalcitrant spouse can repel an entrepreneur's best efforts to communicate and harmonize.

I once had a client with this exact problem. She was the silent brains behind a once-flourishing business that was struggling to meet payroll. Her husband, the nominal face of the business, continued to spend money as if there was absolutely no problem. I had to work around his golf commitments to schedule a meeting with the two of them.

When I sat them down, she explained in great detail the dire financial situation the business was in. He sat there like a spoiled brat, and after his wife finished speaking, he got up and, as he was walking out, said, "I don't want to talk about money. Our business is about helping people. I never was a businessman, I'm a healer!" Not only was he not interested in harmonizing, he wouldn't even acknowledge there was music playing!

Unfortunately, this was clearly a problem that went deeper than the balance sheet. In order to keep peace at home, the client tolerated her husband's childish behavior and absolute refusal to face the truth about their finances. Fortunately, she was a brilliant businesswoman, and we were able to turn the business around while her husband worked on his handicap between occasional visits to the office to pontificate to the staff about how wonderful he was.

It's easy to blame the driven entrepreneur for her inability or unwillingness to harmonize, but sometimes the less involved spouse is the problem. Harmony is a team effort, and not always achievable. When only one person is willing to sing, the best you can hope for is a great solo.

# 13

# TEARS iN AiSLE TWO

*It is better to follow the Voice inside,*
*and be at war with the whole world, than to*
*follow the ways of the world and be at war*
*with your deepest self.*
—Michael Pastore

A FEW YEARS AGO, IN the midst of a devastating personal and professional bankruptcy, I was enveloped by overwhelming misery and shame. My second marriage had fallen apart, and I had just lost all of my money. Again. I had rebuilt my finances with sports and lost it all in real estate.

I hated myself. I had set my life on fire, and was surrounded by the ashes. I was in ruins.

Failure. I was a failure. I couldn't separate the poor business decisions from the person who made them. I was my business, and my business had failed. Case closed. I was a failure. I couldn't see beyond my shame.

I avoided my friends and barely had the energy—or the incentive—to leave the house. The simple act of going to the grocery store was a charade, and I'm a very poor actor. I tried to play the part of a normal person buying groceries.

"Hi, Tom. How are you?"

"I'm fine, Lucy. How are you?"

Such an innocuous, simple exchange; but it took all the courage I could muster to pull it off. One day, very near the absolute bottom for me, I just couldn't do it anymore.

While putting a jar of peanut butter in my cart, I ran into a woman I vaguely knew, who had two young children in tow. I don't recall what she said, but, in response, I burst into tears. I tried to fight it, but I had nothing left.

She briefly tried to console me, while herding her mortified kids toward the safety of the frozen foods section.

I left my cart, walked past the cashiers, got in my car, drove home, closed the door, and cried some more.

Lucy and her kids probably went home and made smoothies.

Why had I done this to myself…again? How could I stop myself from playing this song over and over?

Good questions. The answers didn't come easily, but the search for them led me to a deeper understanding of myself and what I needed to do to avoid another catastrophe.

My real estate failure was Neighborhood Pride, a company I formed to buy, fix up, and sell houses in a declining section of town. I enjoyed the transactional nature of the business, and the lessons I had learned about value and risk/reward ratios while trading commodities served me well in real estate. I was able to spot trends, negotiate effectively, and make a nice profit. The quality of the work was excellent, and the houses were in great shape when I sold them. In the rare cases when I didn't sell them, I rented them to families on government assistance. The cash flow was extraordinary... until it wasn't.

This was before I knew anything about the default industry. The knowledge I gained from that a few years later would have come in handy at this point. Timing is everything.

I knew that most of the people who bought my houses would eventually lose them to foreclosure, just as the people before them had. Mortgages had become so easy to get that people on the fringes of poverty had no trouble getting thirty-year loans at favorable rates. The cycle of economic decline was gaining steam and would leave a wide swath of collateral damage in its wake. My plan was to stay one step ahead of the hurricane.

I knew that what I was doing wasn't right. It was perfectly legal, but not right. People were going to lose their homes, the homes I had sold to them.

I told myself it wasn't my fault. I was buying and selling in the open market at prevailing prices. The quality of my work far exceeded the neighborhood average. My buyers were usually buying the nicest house on their street. They were happy and thanked me profusely. I had guided them through the entire process. More than once, I had been called an angel by a grateful family.

Fallen angel was more like it. The money I was making did not make up for the wrong I knew I was doing. Just because the system was broken didn't mean I had to step in and selfishly reap the rewards of my misbegotten ingenuity.

I now realize that many of the buyers of my homes were just as deep into the scam as I was. They never intended to pay off their loans. Perhaps they told themselves a version of the story I told myself. "Hey, the government is passing out free houses. I'd be a fool not to take one."

Their complicity did not make up for my guilt. I was smart enough to make a living in other ways. Honest ways. No one forced me to start Neighborhood Pride. I did it on my own, for the money. I didn't even see the flippant cynicism in the name. Neighborhood Pride. Yeah, right.

That was the answer. It was impossible for the business to thrive while I, the engine that drove it, was in the midst of such dissonance. My days were spent in complete conflict with my personal values. I had lost sight of who I was and what I stood for. It was only a matter of time before both my business and I collapsed. I couldn't outrun the hurricane.

The mess I had made of my life—divorce and bankruptcy— was the result of living in conflict with my values. In order to recover, I had to come back to the place where my values were in harmony with my actions. I'd been there before, but now I was lost. I needed to find my Pillars of Truth. My time was being spent fighting with myself. And I actually thought I was a pretty good time manager!

You can master all the latest time management apps and fill your calendar with productive meetings and project-related tasks, but if your core values are taking a backseat to short-term gratification, your efforts will be quintessentially counterproductive. I was living proof of that.

As entrepreneurs, we can get so caught up in the chase that our vision becomes clouded. The combination of long hours, haphazard eating habits, and an unrealistic sense of invincibility that comes with the territory can keep us from seeing the impact our work is having on our lives.

My friend, time management expert Amber Vilhauer, is another creative entrepreneur who had to learn this lesson the hard way. Unlike my battle with personal integrity, her health was being brutalized by her work schedule.

In her early twenties, she worked with an international marketing company as a division sales manager. During the busy season, her life consisted of hundred-hour work weeks. For five consecutive months. She thought she was invincible, but her body sent her a powerful wake-up call.

She developed a series of health issues and was forced to dramatically change the way she led her life. Since making her health a top priority, she's created the personal life she always wanted, and, less than ten years later, her business soars to new heights annually.

Her time is efficiently managed with a very rigid work schedule. She works Monday through Friday, generally nine to five. Too many entrepreneurs work around the clock, making it much more challenging to achieve harmony. Our relationships and health tend to suffer the farther we travel down that road.

She also establishes clear boundaries with her clients. They learn early on that she won't reply to emails or requests on nights and weekends unless it's an emergency. Clients know to schedule a call with her, since she doesn't plan for unscheduled calls. They respect her holiday breaks and vacation time.

She says, "It's not that I'm a drill sergeant. In fact, they *love* that I have boundaries, and it usually inspires them to create some boundaries of their own." Of course it does. We are drawn to harmonize with those we admire.

Amber's rituals reflect her dedication to her health and to her husband and growing family. At the end of each workday, she cleans and organizes her desk and then writes her to-do list for the next day. This routine allows her to brain dump all of the tasks and ideas on her mind and leave it all at the office. "When I come home to my family, I get to be fully present because I'm not straining to remember or work through business concerns." That sure sounds like *lifeness* to me.

Amber is, without question, the most productive person I know. When I grow up, I want to be just like Amber.

Another master time manager, one of my teachers, Bruce D Schneider, says, "A common challenge for entrepreneurs is the lack of an effective, working definition of harmony. Entrepreneurs tend to define harmony in terms of short-term parameters, yet with regard to our businesses and our families, it is only achievable through a long-term lens. In this instance, harmony must be seen from a metaview.

"Most entrepreneurs think they don't have enough time, but what they really lack is focus. They need to give each part of their life the attention it needs. Focus, therefore, is the secret to harmony," Bruce explained. "Time shifts when you focus your energy. When you have the discipline to be one hundred percent engaged and connected to where you are at any given moment, and wherever you move to, be there in the same way, then you'll perform better in every aspect of your life."

Bruce suggests that rather than fret over a lack of time to get everything done, one should instead "improve your focus on each task when you are doing it."

Simply put: *Harmony + Focus = Effective Time Management.*

For that formula to work most effectively, you must have buy-in from the key people in your life. By communicating your vision with your spouse, children, friends, and business partners, and by inviting their input, you give them an opportunity to support you in a way that seems collaborative rather than combative.

Bruce suggests asking them:

- What parts of this vision work for us collectively?
- What parts get in the way of what you want?
- What parts enhance what you want?
- What do we need to modify in order to reach our respective and shared goals?

Amber has her rituals, Bruce suggests a focused metaview, Benjamin Franklin had his Thirteen Virtues; I have my Pillars of Truth. You can call them whatever you want. What is important is to identify what you truly stand for as a human being, the non-negotiable values upon which you are unwilling to compromise. Living in harmony with these values is an integral part of a truly productive life. The importance Amber places on her health and family tells you exactly what she stands for.

Shakespeare famously said, "To thine own self be true." Marcus Aurelius put it a different way. "Everything is created for some duty. For what task then, were you created?"

To be true to yourself, as Shakespeare suggests, requires you to know the answer to the question posed by Marcus Aurelius.

Before I could answer that question, after leaving the grocery store in tears, I needed to answer a few more:

- Who am I?
- What are my deeply held spiritual beliefs?
- What do I stand for, without reservation?
- What do I value more than anything else?
- What do I want to achieve in my life?

The answers became my Pillars of Truth. Just like a solid business plan, they are my guides when tough decisions need to be made. The clarity they provide helps me quickly recognize when I'm drifting off course. I could have used them while I was selling houses in "the 'hood."

My Pillars represent all the aspects of my life. Career, health, spirituality, personal growth, family, money, romance, and recreation are examples. You may have others that are specific to you. What matters is that you have them, and live by them.

The Internet and your local bookstore are filled with tools to help organize your day and save time. Some of them are useful, but nothing will keep you more focused and time-abundant than living in harmony with your Pillars of Truth*. The harmonious management of time is an organic process that begins with living your truth. To focus on tightening up your daily calendar is to completely miss the point.

I'll let Amber close out this chapter.

"Achieving harmony IS possible, but it's not easy. Our lives are made up of a series of decisions, rewards, and consequences. The reward of a harmonious life is improved health, relationships, and success. The consequence of a dissonant life is the opposite. All day long we are faced with choices. Give work my full attention, or be distracted. Go home at five or work until eight. The list goes on.

"I focus on the importance of harmony when I make those decisions, and I know that's how I've been able to achieve my biggest goals."

---

* If you'd like to learn the step by step method I used to identify my Pillars, you can download it by visiting www.TomRubens.com/Pillars

# ONE IS A LONELY NUMBER

*Meticulous planning will enable everything
a man does to appear spontaneous.*
—Mark Caine

AFTER THE BANKRUPTCY OF NEIGHBORHOOD Pride, I built a successful real estate brokerage with the help of Bob Corcoran. Bob is widely recognized as one of the true experts in the real estate industry, but he still remembers his early struggles with using his time most efficiently. Bob attributes his extraordinary personal productivity to continually questioning why he does things and the way he does them.

In the early days of his business, Bob would spend ten days on-site at clients' offices, setting up computer systems and training agents in lead generation and management. He also helped his clients create a sustainable organizational culture—one that would encourage growth while keeping all members of the team committed and engaged. Ten days was barely enough time to do this effectively, and he couldn't see any way to condense the training.

Bob recognized that there had to be an easier, more efficient way to deliver his service, but this was the only way he knew, and he was stuck. On the eight-hour drive back to his office after a particularly grueling client visit, Bob decided to evaluate the systems and processes he had in place.

He soon realized three key things that changed the future of his business and his life:

1.  If he continued to work this way, he would soon run out of time and energy to grow his business.
2.  Of the ten days spent on-site, only two days were spent doing things he truly enjoyed.
3.  Much of the work done on-site could be done from his office.

"I broke down each day, and looked for areas where I could be more productive in less time. I saw that the parts of my job that brought me the most joy were the very same parts where I was most efficient, effective and brought the greatest benefit to my clients.

One of my strengths has always been systems. Regardless of the business, I can generally find ways, through systemization, to maximize efficiency. So, my challenge was to apply that skill to my own business!"

By the time he arrived home, he had a plan to reduce the time spent on-site to seven days, with increased productivity. In the intervening years, his billing rate for on-site visits has gone from five thousand to twenty thousand dollars, and the time spent there has been reduced to four. Of course, this allows him to spend more time with his wife, the most important person in his life. Bob works hard, but Brenda has veto power over major business decisions that impact their financial future and time together. That, my friends, is harmony in action.

The essence of the process he used to do this is deceptively simple and has become a key component of his coaching program: "Continually question why you do things and the way you do them. And, above all, remember this: Your whole life changes the moment you make a commitment."

Growth involves change, and effective change evolves from frequent recalibration, based on the best available information. Bob's clients have come to expect him to view their efforts through this lens.

Bob told me the story of a very successful real estate client who told him he wanted to buy a milkshake franchise. Bob knew this would divert the client's attention from his real estate business, and that he was not in the position to run two businesses effectively.

"Serial entrepreneurs are more interested in the hunt. Once they get what they want, they move on to the next thing, and their previous business falters as a result."

When asked why he wanted to buy the franchise, the client told him, "They make great shakes." Bob told him he'd be better off hiring someone whose sole job was to bring shakes to the office every day, rather than shifting attention from his real estate business to run a new business with which he was totally unfamiliar.

Fortunately for the client, he took Bob's advice.

Once the client took the time to reflect on why he wanted to buy the shake franchise and the way he ran his real estate business, the answer was clear. He formed a corporate partnership with the shake shop and now gives gift certificates for free shakes to clients and their families on special occasions.

Bob saw this as "a classic case of an entrepreneur going wide, rather than deep." Going deep is strengthening the foundation of your business, whereas going wide is going outside your area of expertise to seek new opportunity. Wide can work, but not when you have limited time, resources, and experience.

This is a client who thought he knew what he was doing, but he was open to coaching. He allowed the important people in his life to help guide him down the correct path. The ability to harmonize is the hallmark of a great coaching relationship. "So many entrepreneurs make costly mistakes because they think they have to do it all alone. They don't."

When others offer to harmonize with you, accept graciously. Allow those you trust to find your key. Chances are, they'll seamlessly sing over some of your missed notes, and you'll still sound great, even to those in the front row.

# PLAN YOUR WAY TO SUCCESS

*No matter what you do, aim for a goal,*
*so that you have direction. If you're moving*
*towards something, everything you do has a*
*purpose and nothing is a waste of time.*
*Work on enjoying the process.*
*Don't ask for permission. Just do it.*
—Ilana Glazer

ACHIEVING HARMONY IS A TALL order, and we all have moments, sometimes long stretches of our lives, when we just don't measure up. We make poor decisions, abandon the values we thought were most important, and maybe even sabotage our businesses or our families. The resulting pain and guilt cuts as deeply as any wound.

Jay Meyer, a friend and mentor of mine, built a local drugstore into a multimillion-dollar institutional pharmacy business. He and I frequently speak about harmony and the importance of keeping it as a priority in building a business—and a life—of which you can be proud. We've shared some of our own ups and downs, and one of the things that draws us together is our mutual respect for how we've each managed to reset our compasses and use our own mistakes to help others find fulfillment in their businesses and their lives.

Jay's road to success was littered with self-inflicted injuries that almost destroyed his marriage, his career, and the people who mattered most in his life. Recently, he told me, "I can relate to the pain of living a life out of harmony. While I was busy growing my business, I let my commitment to my family and my relationship with my wife flounder. My priorities were so out of whack that I let my softball team take precedence over one of my children's first birthday party. A casual night out with friends was frequently all it took to ignore my wife's health and hurt feelings. My selfishness obscured the things I valued most in the world. Making money and immediate gratification were certainly not core values, but I let them steer my ship right into the eye of a hurricane. I thank God I was able to turn my life around, and that is why I'm so passionate about helping people avoid the mistakes I made."

Jay's road to *lifeness* may have taken some detours, but his roots are firmly planted there now.

Many of the people Jay and I work with have problems planning because they haven't taken time to consider what is most important to them. We discussed two questions to help them get clarity.

First, what is your personal vision (dream with a plan) for your life? Entrepreneurs who have spent years single-mindedly feeding and serving their businesses frequently must face the reality that their personal lives are parched wastelands. This question begins the refocusing process and the search for harmony.

Second, which activities do you need to eliminate, and what personal changes do you need to make, to achieve your vision? As people begin to realize the steep price they have paid for business success, the value of what has been lost comes into sharp focus. We help them find the source of their dissonance. This leads to a conversation about core values, which leads to improved clarity about what steps should be taken next.

Answering these questions leads to the creation of a vision for the future focused upon what is truly important.

Stress is the enemy of harmony, leading many entrepreneurs to failure's doorstep. Clarity and focus offer a powerful antidote. Jay is a very creative, visual thinker, and he drew a chart on my notepad to illustrate this point.

When we lack…
Clarity andFocus
We are left with
Ambiguity and Loss of Control

Which leads to…
Frustration
Which leads to…
Burnout, Stress, Addiction of choice
All of which lead to…
FAILURE

Jay told me, "I can't recall who introduced me to this chart[*]. But I've used it for years. When I see a client struggling to keep his or her life and business afloat, I look at how much of their day is devoted to top priorities. What I frequently see is dissonance and misdirected attention."

The first step toward finding harmony is to regain clarity, and focus on the things that matter most. My goal for each of my clients is that we work together to make the world a better place. I believe that happens by building a harmonic life, one day at a time. This requires a plan.

Just in case you're thinking you'd prefer to just start "doing," rather than waste time "planning," the cost of not having a clear, intentional plan for your business is likely to be far greater than the time and attention you need to spend, right now, to get that plan on paper.

Writing a business plan is frequently a source of fear and stress for entrepreneurs. For some, the pressure of having to put their plan on paper keeps them from writing anything at all.

---

[*] If you know the origin of the chart, please email me at Tom@TomRubens. com. I'd like to give credit in the next edition of *Lifeness*. Thanks!

There is nothing to fear. The goal is to create a road map to use on your entrepreneurial journey—along with your inner personal and moral compass—to help you make important decisions more easily and keep you from being lured off course and distracted from your ultimate purpose. A clear plan will steady your ship when you encounter inevitable rough seas.

Once you are in business, your business plan will serve as a guiding light as you confront tough decisions and course corrections. It is intended to be a living, breathing document, to be modified as products, the marketplace, and customers change.

Carving out a path toward successful entrepreneurship requires planning, strategic vision and, of course, harmony. As you grow, you are likely to need a strategic plan to track the milestones you seek to achieve and the specific steps you'll need to take to keep your business moving forward. This can be a separate document or a part of your business plan devoted to the critical metrics and how you will monitor them. Strategic planning starts with the end in mind and reverse-engineers to the starting point.

I think we'd all agree that a business plan is an essential part of the entrepreneurial toolkit. It provides the melody for the song your business will sing. The best lyrics in the world will remain unsung without a tune to anchor them. Where would Bernie Taupin be without Elton John?

Your business plan is your friend. Take a deep breath and relax. This is the Greatest Hits album of your business: the songs of how you'll make it big and about the obstacles you'll overcome to get there. You'll play this album from time to time to make sure you're on the right track. All you have to do is write the songs*.

---

\* If you'd like my help designing your business plan, head over to TomRubens.com/BusinessPlan. You'll find free tools to help you get started.

# OUTRAGEOUS CULTURE

*"Our number one priority is company culture.
Our whole belief is that if you get the culture
right, most of the other stuff like delivering
great customer service or building a long-
term enduring brand will just happen
naturally on its own."*
—Tony Hsieh

CULTURE TRUMPS EVERYTHING. MORE THAN your product or service, location or strategy, funding or vision, the culture of your business is the most reliable determinant of future success. Your culture is your calling card. A dissonant culture will infect your product or service with a toxicity that could be fatal. A harmonious one, on the other hand, can often overcome seemingly insurmountable obstacles.

Early-stage entrepreneurs and small businesses are particularly vulnerable to the damage just one toxic employee can inflict. When you have ten employees, and one of them is carrying a debilitating virus such as victim energy or profound apathy, the moment the disease spreads to the next employee, you've lost twenty percent of your workforce! A toxic culture will take down the best-engineered product, service, or technology.

Shortly before this book went to press, I encountered a business culture unlike any I had ever witnessed. Walking through the front door felt like entering a warm embrace. The furniture, the art, and the woman behind the front desk all conspired to welcome me like a long-lost friend.

The walls were adorned with photos of employees with their families, tributes to past and current clients, and clear statements about the core values of the company. One that resonated for me was:

*Our sense of family encompasses our homes, our work, and our community.*

Those words ooze harmony.

I saw a closet filled with new toys, coloring books, and other treats for children and pets. Snow days, doctor appointments, and day-care issues are part of life. But they need not be a reason to stay home, especially when your employer creates space in the office for your family. As I walked down a hallway, a healthy-looking guy with a big grin on his face was introduced to me as the "Keeper of the Culture."

Everything about the environment was an invitation to smile.

As a student of corporate culture, I was simply in awe of this company. I asked my guide if I could meet the CEO. "You just did. His other title is Keeper of the Culture." Wow!

A few days later, I was able to spend an hour with Scott McGohan, the CEO and KOTC of McGohan Brabender, one of the largest independent health insurance brokers in the country. We had a wide-ranging conversation about business culture.

I started by asking him about the core value I had seen on the wall on my first visit.

"Family means different things to different people, and the reason we put our definition in that order is this: Our motive toward people is to create better moms and dads, better men and women. When we do that, our business wins and our community wins."

This resonated for me, but I had questions. "What is the price you pay for this culture? Clearly, it costs money to treat people the way you do. I'd guess that some of your competitors have lower employee overhead. How do you overcome this?"

His response was perfect. "First of all, culture is never about money, and it's never about profitability. Great people, fully aligned with your culture, create extraordinary workplace efficiency. When you get everyone in the right lane, doing the right thing, then you don't have to spend much time managing them."

Absolutely. And, when your employees truly believe what you believe, they will handle critical issues exactly as you would. Your culture becomes their guide. That is a harmonious workforce.

"When prospects enter the building, our lives get pretty simple. If you're shopping simply on rate, we're the wrong company for you. But, if you're looking for a partner on the journey, welcome home."

He added, "Two years ago, we told our whole staff, 'We're on a quest for believers, and we want to identify the naysayers, the victims, and the bystanders in the organization. This is what a naysayer says and feels, what a victim says and feels, what a bystander says and feels. As we move forward with our new model, our new vision, if you feel you are one of these people, we're going to give you time. We'll be patient with you, but if you choose to continue to be a naysayer, a victim, or a bystander, there will come a time when we will say you're not the right person for us.'"

Feathers were ruffled. Some people couldn't fully buy in. They were no longer a cultural fit for the company. They couldn't harmonize. Some came to this conclusion on their own, and left to find work elsewhere. Others were let go.

"We did lose a small percentage of our workforce, but we now feel the positive impact the quest for believers had on our culture."

In a business where culture is recognized as a core value, hiring becomes far more than simply looking for great résumés.

"We learn about your college degree and your GPA only if you tell us. Those things are not priorities for us. I'd take one person who's had her teeth kicked in by life before I'd take two who haven't. We hire attitude and train skill."

Agreed. I'd call that hiring to fit your culture rather than to match a job description.

McGohan Brabender's innovative culture encourages authenticity and personal initiative in their employees. The history of the company is filled with stories of employees stepping in to solve a problem for a client in the absence of a specific protocol for the individual issue at hand. For example, when an insurer mistakenly rejected a client's claim, a client support person took her lunch break to drive forty miles to a pharmacy and personally pay for a prescription so that a sick child would not have to go home without her medicine. I'd say that's going way above and beyond.

In *The Artist's Way at Work*, authors Bryan, Cameron, and Allen say, "An individual cannot be truly authentic in an organization that stifles innovation, and an organization cannot be innovative unless the people involved are allowed to be authentic and creative." Those words sound as if they came directly from the McGohan Brabender playbook.

Scott and I didn't discuss health insurance. We talked about the importance of shared values, harmony, and creating an optimal business culture. As a solo practitioner, I'm not a potential client, and Scott didn't try to sell me insurance or convince me of anything. He didn't ask for any leads or referrals. He just shared his vision with a guy he'd recently met. Do you think I will recommend McGohan Brabender to any client or friend in the market for a health insurance broker? Do you think I'll look for every opportunity to share with my tribe the culture Scott and his team have created? I just did.

Throughout my career, from the trading pits to coaching, I've felt that the culture within my organization—even if I was the only person in the organization—was an honest reflection of my core values and beliefs. There have been times, however, (when I was selling homes to people who would have been better off renting, for example) when I was oblivious to or ignoring the facts. Even at my best, I was never as good as Scott and his team at McGohan Brabender.

Evaluating the culture of your business is very difficult to do from the inside, without the help of an impartial observer. One of the challenges I frequently face as a coach is telling a sincere entrepreneur that his problem begins with the culture of which he is so proud. If your business is struggling with personnel, customer service, or sagging revenues, a fresh set of eyes may spot a problem that you are unable to see.

# THE WORLD ACCORDING TO SAM

*Make your choices reflect your hopes,*
*not your fears.*
—Nelson Mandela

ONE NIGHT WHEN SAM WAS about twelve, as I was sitting on the side of his bed kissing him goodnight, he said, "Daddy, tomorrow's going to be a great day."

I replied, "Great, Buddy. What's going on tomorrow?"

"Nothing."

"So, is there something happening at school? An assembly, a fire drill or something cool like that?"

"Nope."

"Plans with Mommy after school?"

"Uh-uh."

"Sam. Tomorrow is Tuesday," I said with a touch of frustration. "What is it about tomorrow that makes it so special?"

"Nothing."

Still not getting it and unready to let go, I prepared for one more round. I mean, really, what could be so great about another day at school? "Sam, if nothing special is going on at school or after school, why is tomorrow going to be such a great day?"

"Because it is."

At this point, looking into his beautiful brown eyes for an answer, it hit me. Hard. Sam had simply decided on Monday night that Tuesday would be a great day. And, of course, it was.

Sam makes this decision every night. He's just wired that way. And he gets just what he expects. Every day.

After our goodnight kiss, I retreated to my bedroom for a few tears and some soul searching. *Why can't I do that? How does he do it?* Of course, the answers were simple. *I could do it, but I don't. He can do it, and he does.*

Sam never really has a bad day. Sure, some are better than others. He doesn't look forward to the dentist any more than the rest of us do, but his focus is always on the good stuff. The free toothbrush.

Currently, Sam works at our local grocery store, Dorothy Lane Market. He couldn't have landed in a better spot. The third generation, family-owned business is known for its outrageously good customer service and community support. We have been shopping there for many years. The company culture embraces diversity, and this job was a dream come true for our whole family.

Ostensibly, Sam was hired to clean tables and empty trash, but he spends as much time socializing with customers and staff as he does doing his actual job. Fortunately for Sam, his quick smile and sunny demeanor are valued by his employers.

Whenever Sam meets someone new, he asks for his or her business card. His wallet is overflowing with cards from friends he's made at work.

For his twenty-fifth birthday, I decided to get Sam his very own business card. As I struggled to come up with a title to put under his name, a friend told me about the original owner of the home that now serves as her office. The poet Helen Steiner Rice, had left behind a dusty box of old books in a corner of the attic. When my friend opened the box, a copy of Ms. Rice's biography, *The Ambassador of Sunshine*, written by Ronald Pollitt, was right on top.

I've never seen him so happy with a gift, but he didn't understand why I would have a card made especially for him. I explained that his new friends would be just as excited to receive his card as he was to receive theirs.

On the front of the card, beneath his picture, are his name and title:

Sam Rubens
Ambassador of Sunshine

"Daddy, why does it say 'Ambassador of Sunshine'? What does that mean?"

"An ambassador is a representative of a person, place, or thing. Do you greet everyone with a smile at work?"

"Yes."

"Do you love your job?"

"Yes."

"Are you happy at work?"

"Yes."

"Your happiness brings a bit of sunshine to everyone you meet, Buddy. That's why you're the Ambassador of Sunshine."

"Okay. That's cool. I understand."

In the years since that night on Sam's bed, I've had some great days and some that have brought me to my knees. I've lost dear friends and made some new ones. I've made money and lost money. Through it all, one thing has remained constant: Sam has had a series of great days.

For the Ambassador, every tomorrow is going to be a great day. I'm still working on that. How about you?

# THE SONG OF SUCCESS

*A man is a success if he gets up in the morning
and goes to bed at night, and, in between,
he does what he wants to do.*
—Bob Dylan

WE ALL HAVE SONGS THAT make up the soundtrack of our lives. Some of these are as uplifting as Aretha coming at you from the front of the church. Hank Williams playing the victim in a minor key sends an entirely different message. The harmony that can be so challenging in our daily lives is second nature when we listen to our favorite songs.

Recently, I was listening to the late Leonard Cohen's "Anthem." As my attention drifted in and out of the music, I realized the chorus was sending me a message I needed to hear. I'd been listening to this song for years, but the message finally hit me like a sliver of sunlight through a crack in the blinds. I guess I was finally ready to hear it.

The words clearly encouraged me to do what I can with what I've got. To look for reasons why I *can* start—release— my project now. To ignore those voices saying that I'm not ready, that I must have everything exactly right before I can take my first steps. Those are simply limiting beliefs. I have all the tools I need to survive—and thrive. I just need to use them.

Maybe he was speaking to you, too. Who said it had to be perfect? That's what first drafts are for. Let your creation breathe. There's no shame in revision. Nike's first running shoes look pretty ridiculous now. If they had waited until they put out the perfect shoe to get into business, we'd still be running around in Bob Cousy's old PF Flyers.

Your clients and customers will have feedback on things that never occurred to you. If you listen, that feedback will help you make your product or service better than you ever dreamed it could be. Just do it!

We deaden our creations by expecting them to be perfect. Perfection isn't possible. Celebrate what you've done! You have the rest of your life to tweak it. Of course you want to do and be your best at all times. We all do. The key is to know that your best is good enough. I love the Navajo tradition of intentionally weaving one small flaw into their beautiful rugs to give any evil spirits residing in the rug a way to escape. Let go of toxic fears. Embrace your unique contribution and honor your entrepreneurial spirit.

Welcome the light peeking through the blinds. It comes to shine on your creation. You are an entrepreneur. You are, by definition, a creator. Give thanks for the cracks, the imperfections, the challenges. Trust. Believe. They are there for a reason.

What songs are you singing today? Are they in harmony with the soundtrack of your intentions? The songs we sing to ourselves can become an inner dialogue. If you have a big idea that's been incubating long enough, sing it out. Make it your anthem. Harmonize.

19

# AN UNEXPECTED CHANGE IN PLANS

*Being ready isn't enough.*
*You have to be prepared.*
—Pat Riley

SATURDAY WAS SUPPOSED TO BE my big day. The first installment of my new radio show, *The Accountability Factor Radio Hour*, would be live at four p.m. I was excited, proud, and ready. For the past three months, I had worked on the show and looked forward to the moment when I would begin presenting weekly inspiration, guidance, and expert guests' perspectives to entrepreneurs and small business owners seeking to get the most out of their businesses and their lives.

I'd been coaching for less than a year, and the radio show was my first attempt to gain traction for the business. I wasn't confident in my abilities and I was particularly sensitive to how I was perceived. Of course, this limited my ability to be spontaneous and be myself.

I had named my business The Accountability Factor. It sounded strong, and I needed a powerful name to hide my insecurity. It took nearly four years before I rebranded and changed the name of my business to Tom Rubens Business Coaching.

Now I can confidently offer my services, knowing that the value I bring to my client's business far exceeds the fees I charge. On my first day in the studio, however, I wasn't so self-assured.

My guests were in the studio, eager to share their stories. Friends and family were tuned in. I had pages and pages of notes and reminders to help me relax and overcome the anxiety I felt about my debut.

I had notes for every possible eventuality. What if the guests don't show up? Got that covered with an extra feature. What if the taped interview I did with a successful local businessperson was accidentally erased? No problem, I'll just talk about his book and how much can be learned from his experiences.

Nothing was going to shake me up. I was ready for anything. And then, of course, the unexpected happened. About two minutes before we were to go on the air, the producer informed me that he would be cutting away to a live press conference from Aurora, Colorado. The governor, the local police chief, and the FBI would be giving more details about the horrible tragedy that had occurred at a local movie theater just a couple nights earlier. The producer wasn't sure when the conference would begin, so he told me to start the show, but expect to be cut off as soon as the press conference began.

I went from "all systems go" to mortified, in the blink of an eye. Should I race through my intro and get as much of it out as possible? Introduce myself to the audience and tell them about our new show and then wait until the horrific details of a national tragedy were replayed before starting the fun?

I think the technical term for what I experienced in that moment is discombobulation. My cool was completely blown. I had to show my compassion for the victims and their families while trying to stick to my plan to deliver an inspirational show. This was live radio; I had no time to regroup. Maybe, if I'd had just a bit more experience, I would have been able to handle the situation better. Or perhaps if I had given my plan some flexibility, I would have been prepared for a detour.

I panicked. Despite all my planning, I had left no room for life to intervene. I blew it.

Life is much more like jazz, with crazy solos and occasional detours, than a symphony, in which every part is played the same way with each performance. Great artists may have general ideas when they sit down to create, but the finished work frequently looks or sounds completely different from what they originally had in mind. The key is trust. A John Coltrane solo might stretch the limits of a song's tether, but his bandmates knew he'd always find his way back to the melody.

Our businesses are like that, too. We don't live in a vacuum, and the events we encounter are frequently out of our control. Being prepared is important, but being flexible is essential for those times when your plan needs a tweak on the fly. Your business plan will be your guide through good times and bad. Remember, however, it is not written in stone.

A couple days after what I had been thinking of as "the debacle," I received an email from the radio station, with a link to the show. To my surprise, it wasn't as bad as I thought. Whew! Apparently I was a little hard on myself, another staple of the entrepreneurial personality. In our hyper-focused pursuit of success, it's easy to miss the opportunities presented by the jazz of life.

Entrepreneurs are creators, and sometimes we let our inner critic overwhelm our precious creations. Be kind to yourself during the creative process. As your business evolves, and you evolve with it, there will be times when you don't do everything right. You will make mistakes. Be prepared to forgive yourself and continue dancing to the altered tune.

My life is far more harmonious now than at any earlier time in my life, but I'm still a work in progress. While I've reset my compass for loftier goals, it's still a challenge to show up as the best version of myself every day. The good news is that I know the drill. I know what I need to do to get where I'm headed. And so do you.

# LEADERSHIP AND THE CULTURAL IMPERATIVE

*The only thing of real importance that*
*leaders do is to create and manage culture.*
—Edgar Schein

I MADE THE TRANSITION FROM real estate investor to real estate agent around the time my business filed for bankruptcy. I had an email account, a cell phone, and a car. Bingo. I was back in business. Quickly, I was overwhelmed with work, so I rented an office and hired the first person with a pulse willing to start immediately.

Since I was busy and didn't take the time to train her, Ellen had to figure everything out on her own. She did just that. However, because I had neglected to clearly communicate to her my values and the mission of our company, she made decisions and did things based on her own values.

For example, Ellen didn't think it was important to return phone calls or even answer the phone when she was busy with other tasks. She treated our clients as if they were annoying distractions keeping her from doing her work. I saw clients as the reason I do the work and the source of my income. Their satisfaction was the measuring stick of my success.

Shame on me for not paying attention until it made an impact on the bottom line, by which time clients were already upset. I would have fired myself, if I could.

Creating the culture of your company is the most important thing you can do while your business is in the embryonic stage, and the best time to do this is *before* you hire your first employee. Changing your culture after it has been infected by a toxic employee is far more difficult than creating a healthy culture in the first place. Mistakes, at this stage, can be fatal for your business.

I violated one of the first rules of management: *Inspect what you expect.* Don't assume your instructions are being followed simply because you set the expectation. Inspect. Regularly.

Gradually, I was able to steer Ellen to the path I had in mind, but the damage had been done. She felt I had undermined her, and my "suggestions" were seen as micromanagement. Her attitude took a nosedive. A cancer had formed.

Attitude shift notwithstanding, I needed her desperately, which led me to make another critical mistake: I let her keep her job and I hired my second employee. Of course, Ellen infected him, and the result threatened to destroy my business.

Now the problem had metastasized, and I needed to take immediate action. My dilemma was this: If I fired Ellen without first finding a replacement, I would be forced to do her job while doing my own *and* while finding and training a new employee. We were each working ten-hour days, so that would be an enormous burden for me. If I kept her around long enough to train her replacement, I would risk the probable infection of the new hire, before that person had a chance to absorb our culture.

Neither option was appealing, but the choice was clear. I had hired Ellen out of despair and hadn't trained her properly. I could not afford to make those mistakes again. The short-term easy way out carried with it a virtual long-term guarantee of failure. So, she had to go. Immediately.

My other employee was still salvageable, but he needed to see me take decisive action; otherwise, he might reasonably assume that Ellen's behavior was acceptable.

I called my customers, explained the situation, and asked for their patience. I told them, "I'll be understaffed for a short time while we retool our infrastructure and temporarily unable to meet the high standards you've come to expect. I suggest you send some business to my competitors until I'm fully staffed."

Most customers/clients will respect your honesty, give you every opportunity to fix the problem, and welcome you back when you say you're ready. In this way, you've actually used a problem—and your approach to its solution—to demonstrate your commitment to the culture and values of the company.

With the protection and promotion of your precious culture as a priority, the hiring process becomes more clearly defined. You are no longer willing to hire out of need; instead you hire only those who embrace your culture. Skills can be learned. You can train someone to operate a machine or run a new computer program. But you can't train someone to believe what you believe.

By conveying your expectations clearly and decisively, your new hires will know exactly how to handle a situation in your absence. It is essential that every employee buy in to your culture without reservation. Once there are two or more of you, this culture becomes your bond. Decision-making is easier when you have a compass—a culture—to guide you.

Corporate culture can be succinctly defined as "the way we do things around here." Leadership is the act of controlling or directing others. In biology, symbiosis describes the relationship, generally advantageous to both parties, between two different organisms living in close proximity to each other.

Can an effective business culture exist without leadership? No. Can a leader exist in the absence of culture? No. Is each enhanced by the strength of the other? Yes. Therefore, within the most successful organizations there exists a symbiotic relationship between culture and leadership.

In the case of a start-up or owner-operated small business, the founder, knowingly or not, creates the culture of the business. The success of that business is directly related to the quality of the culture she creates. Or, said another way, the success of a leader is dependent on the degree to which he creates, embraces, and nurtures the company culture.

Seth Godin said, "Your brand is the promise you make." The same is true of your culture. Keeping that promise to both employees and customers is non-negotiable.

More than your product or service, location or strategy, funding or vision, the culture of your business is the most reliable determinant of future success. Correspondingly, the leader's passion must be in alignment with the culture of the company, team, or organization she is expected to lead.

As the company grows, the authority vested in the leader emanates from her profound commitment to embracing the culture of the organization. A successful leader will have the following four traits:

1. A seamless alignment between her core values and the culture of the organization.
2. The courage to innovate and initiate bold action in the face of great risk.
3. The ability to attract, inspire, and motivate a core group of followers (future leaders) who share her passion for and commitment to the company culture.
4. An unwavering commitment to expect and exemplify clarity and accountability.

The culture of a business is the flag all employees, managers, and executives are committed to defend. Loyalty to the flag is an absolute requirement for employment. The best leaders create such a powerful "why" around the mission behind the culture that employees see their work as a heroic journey toward an honorable goal.

Toward what goal can the leader direct his team without a clearly defined culture? Really, without a flag or coordinates by which to chart a course, what use is there for a leader? In a business with multiple layers of management, effective leaders are key drivers of overall success. Leaders are not attracted to a vacuum. A powerful "why" will attract powerful leaders. The culture must reflect that "why."

When working with leaders, I begin by examining the relationship between the culture of the company and the core beliefs of the individual. These must be in alignment, because any conflict observed by the followers will undermine the leader's ability to lead.

Sometimes, in small-to-medium-sized businesses, the entrepreneur/owner/founder is particularly skillful in providing the product or service on which the company was founded, but unaware of the critical importance of formulating a coherent company culture. As the business grows, the lack of a clearly articulated and universally accepted company culture can be debilitating and, occasionally, fatal.

A mid-level manager is at a severe disadvantage in the absence of a companywide understanding of, and agreement with, the cultural foundation of the organization. When support and clarity are not forthcoming from above, managers in this position must establish a culture within their team to create the uniformity of purpose needed to accomplish their assigned mission. This is an excellent test of leadership skills and it may ultimately serve as a referendum on the viability of the enterprise.

With the desire for a harmonious relationship between the workplace and home in mind, the four traits of a successful corporate leader mentioned earlier in this chapter, with a few subtle changes, are also a guide to effective parenting.

1. Live in seamless alignment with the values you would like to pass along to your children and share with your spouse.

2. Model the courage to be different, to create and honor your unique identity, and to understand that the greatest risk is to sacrifice your truth for the instant gratification of "fitting in with the crowd."

3. Inspire and motivate your family to share your passion for and commitment to your core values.

4. Maintain an unwavering commitment to expect and exemplify clarity and accountability.

If you say you'll be home for dinner, but frequently call at the last minute to say you're stuck in a client meeting, the contradiction between your words and behavior will sabotage the "family first" value you want to instill. What message does that send about your commitment to your word? To your agreement to share parenting duties? When you tell your kids how much you love them, but fail to show up for the school play, the big game, or the piano recital, what does that say about your values and priorities? Your integrity? Your committment to Lifeness?

Taking your family on a camping trip while your neighbors boast of their five-star hotel in Hawaii illustrates your belief that developing a relationship with nature is more important than returning from spring break with a sweet suntan. Sharing your love of learning and spiritual exploration shows your family how much you value education and an open mind. Sharing your enthusiasm for helping others who are less fortunate by spending a beautiful spring day feeding the homeless in a crowded shelter will leave an indelible mark on the lives of your children. Coaching soccer or leading a scout troop will introduce your kids to leadership in action.

Your commitment to clarity in words and actions is a powerful illustration of leadership for your family. The feeling of security that comes from knowing what is expected of them and what they can expect from you, will lead to better decision-making and more self-confidence for your children. Clarity will strengthen your relationship with your spouse and build a powerful foundation of trust for your children to witness.

In the same way middle managers utilize well-defined cultures to lead their teams, your children will thrive when grounded in a culture they understand and can rely on. With that as their foundation, they will learn to confidently lead their little brothers and sisters, classmates and friends, while developing into the type of people who will inspire future generations.

Starting a family and starting a business require many of the same skills. The lessons learned from raising a family will help you sell widgets. The strategies you use to inspire your employees are valuable tools for the parental toolbox.

# MARRAKESH EXPRESS REVISITED

*If your actions inspire others to dream more,*
*learn more, do more, become more,*
*you are a leader.*
—John Quincy Adams

IN MY EARLY THIRTIES, DURING a backpacking trip through Spain, I decided to take a detour and explore Morocco. While I was there—thanks to Graham Nash—I decided to ride the train from Casablanca to Marrakesh, The Marrakesh Express. My memory of the experience is a bit vague, but I think I had a pretty good time.

Nearly thirty years later, shortly after I formed the real estate brokerage firm and opened the first office in Cincinnati, I had the opportunity to return to Morocco for an extraordinary leadership retreat. This journey began, as so many heroic tales do, in a land far, far away: Dayton, Ohio. Yes. Dayton, Ohio. I was sitting at my desk, in an office I had grown to hate, when I received a call from my friend Trebbe, who had guided me on my first vision quest. She and fellow guide Eugene Hughes were taking an international group of business and community leaders on a journey to explore the limits of their skills and abilities and dig deeper into the depths of their own longings. There had been a cancellation, and Trebbe asked if I wanted to join them. In Morocco. In two weeks.

I love Trebbe, but I wasn't in the mood for more spiritual archaeology, and this sounded as if it might actually be hard work. Further, I was no longer a big fan of international travel, and flying to Morocco on short notice was not at all appealing. Nonetheless, with some trepidation, I agreed to join the group, primarily because of Trebbe's power of persuasion and my faith in her skills as a guide.

My fear of air travel within Morocco, coupled with my misguided desire to retrace the steps of a decidedly non-spiritual trip I had taken decades earlier, led me to fly to Casablanca and then take the train to Marrakesh. This was one of those ideas that sounded really good at the time, but the practical application was not what I'd had in mind.

First of all, I had completely forgotten what an impatient, finicky, pain-in-the-butt tourist I am. Second, I had also failed to consider the inherent difficulties of international travel for one who is intellectually incapable of learning more than "thank you" and "where's the bathroom" in any other language. Additionally, I ignored the reality that lugging an overstuffed backpack in oppressive heat was no longer on my bucket list.

Changing planes in Lisbon was an experience I'd rather forget, my room in Casablanca smelled worse than a moldy Midwest basement in July, and by the time I made it to the train station I was thoroughly exhausted and at least two shots of tequila away from calming down.

I boarded the train just as it was leaving the station. There were no seats left, so I sat on my backpack in the airy space between cars, among a group of men determined to smoke every cigarette they had with them during our lovely ride. This wasn't exactly the soundtrack of my last trip down these tracks.

After about an hour or so, just as I had come to appreciate my open-air seating arrangement, the conductor came by and told me I had to find a seat. At least I think that's what he said as he motioned down the aisle of the car, pointed to me and my backpack, and gave the universal "shuffle off to Buffalo" sign.

I meekly did as I was told, while my smoking friends held their ground. Walking down the aisle, looking into compartments filled with people eating food I didn't recognize while speaking a language I didn't understand, I felt like a freak. I wasn't happy and I just wanted to be back at my toxic office in Dayton. When I came upon a compartment with an empty space, I sat down and prepared to be miserable for the balance of the train ride.

Fortunately for me, the universe had other plans.

The entire tenor of my trip, and perhaps the rest of my life, changed when I was jolted from my childish pouting by the words, in perfect English, "Is there room for me to sit next to you?" Nourelhouda, a twenty-five-year-old Moroccan woman with saintly brown eyes, was looking directly at me. Instantly, I knew I was in the presence of a gifted leader.

As Nourellhouda—and her younger sister, Rajae—settled in, our now very cozy compartment became filled with light and laughter. I had been so caught up in my own pity party that I'd failed to notice the faces of the others sitting with me. Suddenly we became a celestial community, orbiting around our sun, Houda.

Houda was returning home from a doctor's visit. Rajae was along to provide love and physical support. Since being diagnosed with multiple sclerosis, Houda had been making this trip regularly. Although she faced an uncertain future and was feeling the effects of both the medication and the disease, Houda distributed her love freely and without hesitation.

Houda demonstrated one of the key traits of a leader: She brought out the best in others. She listened with the ears of her heart and responded with warm empathy toward all. Each of us felt as though we were seen and heard, and responded in kind. Thus a bond was formed, created by an extraordinary woman.

Without a trace of self-pity, Houda told of the challenges she faced and the strength she derived from her faith. By acknowledging her vulnerability, Houda demonstrated the courage she would need to stay strong while confronting her illness.

Time flew by as we shared our stories, laughed, and even shed a few tears. As we talked of work, family, love, and things both simple and grand, I knew this experience would be forever woven into the fabric of my life. Houda taught me about trust, understanding, patience, and faith simply by opening her heart on a crowded train. She embodied the leadership skills I sought.

But this was not a one-way street. I also had a powerful impact on Houda. In me, she had encountered a man who saw her for the beautiful gift of light she truly was, a man who honored her ability to empower others while staying positive in the face of ongoing physical challenges.

Houda knew nothing of the pathetic sniveling cretin whose descent into his own personal hell she had so perfectly interrupted. What she saw was the man I had inside me, the man I knew I could be, the man I was becoming, the man writing these words, a leader in training.

I had come to Morocco to learn about leadership from two respected guides, yet here I was learning at the feet of a young woman on her way home from a doctor's appointment. A ride that had earlier seemed as if it would last forever was now over in a flash. Too soon, it would be time for us to part and go our separate ways. I was headed to the High Atlas Mountains to join my guides, and fellow seekers, Houda and Rajae, were going home to their family. Each of us was markedly changed by our glorious chance encounter.

Less than forty-eight hours removed from Dayton, saying goodbye on the train platform, I was jolted by Houda's parting words. "Tom, are you on Facebook?"

The compression of personal distance on our twenty-first century planet is astounding. I could actually keep in touch with Houda? On Facebook? That hadn't occurred to me, but of course she has a computer, a cell phone, and a Facebook account. Why wouldn't she?

As I watched Houda and Rajae fade into the swarm of people, I felt flush with love and inspiration and grateful for the abundant gifts from an unexpected guide. Houda is a leader, and the lessons we exchanged would serve us both as we continued on our travels.

My leadership journey began, with help from Houda, on a crowded train in a foreign land. It took a train ride halfway around the world to clear the cobwebs obscuring my path toward leadership, but the lessons are everywhere. We just have to be open to receiving them.

# SPENDING THE DAY WITH REGRET

*Fear… Don't ignore it. It will never ignore you.*
—Marsha Marsh

ON THE LEADERSHIP RETREAT THAT followed my Marrakesh Express adventure, an intrepid band of seekers and I experienced the natural beauty surrounding the Kasbah du Toubkal in the spectacular High Atlas Mountains of Morocco. We also explored the inner landscape of our hearts. We learned about leadership from the river, the mountains, our guides, and gracious Berber villagers. My heart expands with warmth just typing these words.

The opportunity to explore deep inside myself holds endless fascination for me. I never really know what I'll find—and sometimes it isn't pretty–but I know I'll be richer for the journey.

I chose to spend one particularly hot day alone, exploring my experience with regret. That may sound dark and depressing, but it was nothing of the sort. The result of regret can be sadness or guilt, but I was more interested in examining the actions I had taken or not taken that led to the feeling of regret. I had no idea where this quest would lead, but I was drawn to revisit the moments in my life in which regret played a part.

Shortly after sunrise, I found a spot on the side of a hill among the rocky remains of what was once a simple shelter, perhaps for small animals. Offering scant protection from the sun and wind, and with walls only three feet high and no roof, my chosen location would leave me exposed to extreme heat for the better part of the day. Nonetheless, I saw it as a safe place to open my heart and explore.

I began by writing down every regret I could remember, with the intention of inviting each experience to join me for a reunion. I expected to write pages and pages documenting years of regret, but the guest list turned out to be manageable. The intimacy of the gathering surprised me.

Many moments I had regretted at the time had actually been part of a larger plan. When I understood that, rather than feeling regret, I was actually grateful for the experiences.

Looking at the smaller than expected assemblage, I searched for a theme. Was there a thread woven into each of my regrets? Could I identify a behavior common to the majority of the experiences? Yes. And, yes.

The overwhelming majority of my regrets were for things I didn't do, the risks I didn't take, the opportunities I allowed to pass me by, and the vulnerabilities I didn't expose. Of course, I've done some things I regret, but most of the guests at this party were challenges I didn't accept rather than failures or shame related to actions I had taken.

Risks and opportunities not taken that could have led to great success, were the source of abundant regret. Why was my life filled with so many unopened gifts?

This one hit me hard. There was no way around it. What had held me back time and time again? Why had I stayed on the sidelines when I could have been in the game? One thing: Fear. Overwhelming fear.

Each time I had stopped short of my goal, it had been fear that held me back. Fear of loss, fear of pain, fear of embarrassment, fear of failure—even fear of success.

I thought I'd be spending the day with regret, but fear had just crashed the party.

My first reaction was sadness—sadness for all the experiences I missed because I was afraid of the consequences. Fortunately, the sadness didn't last long. It gave way to excitement, because I knew that I had found a powerful ally in my fight to avoid future regret.

No evidence supported my fear of action. My regret was born in a stew of inaction. Armed with this clarity, I saw how I could use my fear to serve me rather than inhibit me.

We must learn to turn fear into an asset rather than a liability.

Early stage entrepreneurs, almost-preneurs, wishiwasa-preneurs, and even experienced business owners most commonly cite lack of money as the reason for turning back from, rather than facing the challenge of starting or expanding their business. I'm not buying that! Fear keeps more potential success stories on the sidelines than lack of money ever could.

Being broke is no excuse. In fact, it can be the ultimate motivator. Daymond John, in *The Power of Broke*, puts it best. "If you let broke beat you down, you'll never find a way to thrive, or even survive. But if you look broke in the face, if you define it, own it, make it part of who you are and how you go about your business… well, then you've got something." Now, that's how you turn fear into an ally. "Own it."

Fear is frequently the first demon that rises up to stop us in our tracks on the way to our dreams. For some, the fear of failure is overwhelming; it is almost paralyzing. We get so busy replaying an old story, that we find ourselves stuck with the belief that failing at something makes us a failure. Wrong! Staying inside our comfort zones might be the surest guarantee of failure I know.

Interestingly, the fear of success is sometimes even more powerful than the fear of failure. If this is an issue for you, check in with yourself regarding money. What does money mean to you? Do you have negative beliefs about wealthy people? Are you afraid of who you'll become when you achieve great wealth?

As entrepreneurs, we're all vulnerable to fear, yet sometimes fear is just a reminder to pay attention. Are you afraid to take that next step toward starting your business? To try something that's never been done? To bring a new product to market? Just check in with yourself and make sure this fear is not based on a limiting belief such as, "I'm not ready to own my own business," or "Who am I to start something completely different?"

Giving in to fear will put you in the position to look back on the past with regret. Don't make the same mistake I made. Embrace your fears—whatever they may be—and run directly toward the biggest version of yourself you can imagine.

Every single regret I encountered on the side of that mountain could have been avoided if I had been strong enough and wise enough to look my fear in the eye and say, "Thank you for the warning, but I'm going for it!"

It's time for you to make an ally of an old adversary.

## 23

# THE LOYAL SOLDIER

*War is over! If you want it!*
—John Lennon

SIMPLY BECOMING AN ENTREPRENEUR IS a courageous act. In many cases, it requires listening to all the reasons "it won't work" from well-meaning friends and family. Stories of how most businesses fail and why, will probably be part of the chorus. Sailing through this sea of doubters can be a daunting test of your convictions.

Sometimes, however, the biggest challenge requires overcoming a dialogue that has been going on inside your head for years. The voice behind these well-meaning words goes by many names. The one that resonates most for me is "The Loyal Soldier."

Hiroo Onoda was a Japanese Army Intelligence officer during World War II. He was stationed on Lubang, a long narrow island about a hundred miles southwest of Manilla. The last order from his superiors came in early 1945, when he was told to stay and fight. Never surrender. The final words he heard from his commanding officer were, "Whatever happens, we'll come back for you."

Later that year, after the Japanese had surrendered, while hiding in the jungle Lieutenant Onoda and three other soldiers read leaflets dropped from the sky announcing the end of the war. Assuming they were propaganda, the men kept their rifles at the ready while stealing food from villagers to survive. More leaflets were dropped, this time with pictures and letters handwritten by the soldiers' family members, begging them to come home. Still, they suspected trickery.

Onoda had extensive training in guerilla warfare, survival, and counter-intelligence. He was trained to always be on the lookout for false messengers. It was his duty to be suspicious of any message he received that could not be absolutely verified. Leaflets, letters, and even family photos could easily be doctored. He was not about to be fooled by such simple tactics.

Occasionally, when the men were moving about the jungle, they would find newspapers and personal messages left intentionally for them to find. They read the stories, saw the photos of Japan, and believed them to be placed there by the enemy. They evaded and occasionally attacked and killed members of search parties sent to tell them to come home, the war was over. These men were still at war. The increasing mountain of evidence must be false.

One of Lieutenant Onoda's men left the group and surrendered in 1950, and another died in a gunfight with the Philippine police a few years later. Even when he received word from the soldier who surrendered, confirming the war was over, he persevered. Lieutenant Onoda was not leaving his post absent orders. Unimpeachable orders. Verified orders.

The remaining two men lived in the jungle, stealing rice and clothing, and even cows on occasion, from villagers in the valley below. At no time did they waver from their commitment to the war. Of course, they did have moments of doubt, but, in their minds, none of the evidence was sufficient to confirm that the war was over.

In 1959, Onoda recognized the voices of his brother and sister calling to him over loudspeakers blaring from the valley below. He was able to get close enough to see their faces, but convinced himself that the affair was staged as part of a nefarious American plot.

He read about the Summer Olympics in Tokyo in 1964 and rationalized that The Games could be held in the midst of a World War. By this time, he was unable to understand anything that did not match his own well-worn, but chronically incorrect beliefs. He steadfastly fought his own war, ignoring all evidence that the war he was sent to fight had long since been over.

In 1965, the soldiers found a radio in a villager's hut while pillaging it for food and clothing. They would listen to broadcasts from Japan and assumed they were edited by the enemy and rebroadcast to reflect only what the Americans wanted them to hear.

Lieutenant Onoda's final comrade was killed in 1972 in an ambush on a supply run. Alone, he vowed not to die without a fight. He was at war. His final orders were, "Never Surrender." His integrity was not negotiable. He would die before dishonoring his country.

In 1974, Lieutenant Onoda was found by a Japanese student who told him the war really was over. Of course, he didn't believe him and sent the student away. Within a couple months, the young man returned with a delegation from Japan, including Onoda's former commanding officer, the man who had given him his last order, nearly thirty years earlier.

In his full military uniform, this long-retired Army Major presented Lieutenant Hiroo Onoda with his new orders and relieved him of duty.

The Loyal Soldier finally agreed to leave his post. He turned over his sword, his rifle, several hand grenades, and a dagger his mother had given him to use to kill himself in case he was captured.

Fifteen years after he was declared legally dead, and twenty-nine years after the Japanese surrendered, The Loyal Soldier returned home to a hero's welcome.

On the one hand, this is a story of unwavering loyalty in spite of long odds and personal sacrifice. Seen from another perspective, however, these four brave men ignored the truth and spent years defending ground that had already been surrendered. For nearly three decades, Lieutenant Onoda and his men fought a war that existed only in their heads.

I first heard this story on a Vision Quest in the wilderness of southeastern Utah, and tears flooded from my eyes. What a tragedy! These men stubbornly wasted a huge chunk of their lives. For nothing. Their refusal to accept the truth left them living like savages in the jungle for nearly thirty years!

But my tears weren't only for the soldiers and their families and friends. I cried with the realization that this was the story of my life.

I thought of the wars I had been fighting with my parents, teachers, and virtually anyone in a position of authority. Absent a complete apology and admission of guilt, I'd steadfastly refused to forgive anyone who had ever wronged me. I couldn't stop thinking about the heaviness of carrying around a backpack overflowing with profound anger for over half my life.

I have a Loyal Soldier inside me. He's been there since early childhood. His initial mission was to insure my survival, and he did that. However, as I got older, he kept me stuck in a perpetual state of adolescent confusion and rage.

We all have an internal Loyal Soldier whose sole purpose is our protection. He doesn't want us to get hurt. He wants to keep us safe. He does this by warning us of danger: *Don't dive into shallow water. Remember to bring an umbrella. Don't drink and drive.* Great advice, but occasionally our Loyal Soldier is wrong.

*Don't quit your job and risk your life savings on a new business. That's a terrible location for an Italian restaurant. Don't go into retail; your employees will rob you blind.* Following advice like this can keep us from reaching for our dreams. It can stifle the energy we need to move forward with confidence.

Our Loyal Soldier witnessed our childhood traumas. He saw us cry with heartbreak. He felt pain when we were rejected and hurt. He knows where our shame is hidden and where our fear resides. He wants to save us from any anguish and loss. He means well, and this is the only way he knows to take care of us.

Unfortunately, for some of us, his presence has kept us imprisoned.

With the best of intentions, he inundates us with limiting beliefs. He tells us we aren't worthy of the lofty goals we've set. He does this because he's seen us cry when our dreams were crushed and he doesn't want that to ever happen again. In his mind, the best solution is to avoid big dreams.

By smothering our creativity and charisma, he keeps us from the risk of the rejection and humiliation he believes will come if we fully express our greatness. Unfortunately, his protection keeps us from truly growing up.

And, let's be clear. He has no intention of leaving his post.

For us to cross the bridge from spiritual adolescence to adulthood, he must surrender, and we must make peace with him.

Lieutenant Onoda returned home to parades and an outpouring of gratitude from the Japanese people. They honored him for his service and facilitated his successful return to his community.

Of course, it took him a while to overcome his confusion.

His countrymen had already accepted that they lost the war. They'd moved on to create one of the healthiest economies in the world. Their previously hated rivals, the enemy they had sworn to defeat, were now their trading partners. People weren't walking around with bowed heads in solemn despondence. On the contrary, they were happily living their lives.

Over time, with the support of his friends and family, Lieutenant Onoda came to accept this new version of Japan.

It's the same with our Loyal Soldier. We must honor and thank him for his selfless dedication to our safety. He needs to feel our gratitude for helping us survive adolescence. Most importantly, we must help him find a new role to play in our future.

I've named my Loyal Soldier Elliot. He warns me about taking too much risk. He reminds me of my past failures. He loves me and gives me advice he truly believes to be in my best interest. He has a pretty bad temper and sometimes loses it when he feels I'm under attack. I know he represents the part of me that needs to feel safe and secure.

I've made peace with Elliot. We've learned to work with each other. His voice will always be heard, but I no longer accept his limiting beliefs as truth. I know playing small doesn't serve me, so when I'm overcome with a wave of self-deprecation and fear, I thank him for his concern and remind him that when I encounter setbacks, I can handle them on my own. I won't let short-term failure define me.

Occasionally, I'll take his advice, but he knows the final decision is mine. I've chosen the entrepreneurial life. I appreciate Elliot's vigilance. But we both know, I'm driving the bus.

Whatever road you choose, whether it's being an artist, an entrepreneur, or a valued employee, your success in life will depend upon the degree to which you are able to acknowledge and honor your Loyal Soldier, while staying true to who you are.

That's no easy task. I understand. There will be moments of fear and doubt, but you need not succumb to them. Use your own strength and dedication to overcome whatever roadblocks appear on your journey.

Keep your Loyal Soldier* as a trusted ally in adulthood. His acute sense of imminent danger is a valuable early warning system. Just make sure to fact-check the information he gives you. Doubts can be credible warnings of unnecessary risk. But they can also pose as fears—unwarranted fears of leaving the safety of your comfort zone.

Most importantly, lay down your arms. They no longer serve you. In fact, they are specifically designed to keep you from enjoying a life of maximum productivity, personal growth, and the realization of your dreams.

Elliott and I wish you all the best.

---

* To learn more about your Loyal Soldier visit www.TomRubens.com/LoyalSoldier

# 24

# OLD FRIENDS

*Lord when all my work is done*
*Bless my life and grant me one*
*Old friend at least one old friend*
—Roger Miller

I RECENTLY CELEBRATED YET ANOTHER birthday. As birthdays go, this one was rather uneventful. I worked most of the day, had a couple meetings, heard from a few Facebook friends, received some birthday phone calls, and that was about it. I'd had dinner the night before with Sam.

The day passed, and I was fine with tacking another year onto my résumé. That evening, a new friend was visiting my home and noticed a framed letter on the wall. She read the letter and began to cry. I knew what she was reading. It has hung in a place of honor for many years, but it had been quite a while since I took the time to really read it. It is a birthday letter from a dear friend, written to me more than ten years earlier.

Our friendship began in kindergarten and survived high school, a stint in the army (me, not him), college, marriages, kids, divorces (mine, not his), and business successes and failures. All the while, our friendship thrived. There was never a moment when we weren't friends. Close friends.

The cherished events in our lives were shared. Our children learned about friendship by observing us. Our spouses honored the bond we had, knowing that the men they married had been shaped by the boys we once were.

When my visitor left, I took the letter down from the wall and reread it. And then I cried, too.

I cried in gratitude, for I know the precious gift of friendship is not given to all. I cried for the simple joy of knowing that there will always be someone near who knows the me who lives in the warm memories of the summers of our youth. I cried because there is someone who knows how hard I've worked to become the man I am today… someone who loved me even when I was struggling just to stay alive.

Mostly though, I cried because Larry is gone. Because I miss him. Because right in the middle of the letter, he wrote, "Old friends reach milestones together, cheering on the other, side by side." And now, as I reach for new milestones in my life, Larry is not here to cheer me on. Even more importantly, he is not here to cheer on his children—Dan, Molly, Sam, and Bennett—as they begin their journeys. He is not here to grow old with Debbie, the love of his life. He left us to reach our milestones without him.

Our birthdays are twenty-seven days apart, and although we knew how special we were to each other, our birthdays always gave us another chance to embrace the joy that only old friends can truly share. Many of the special moments and landmark birthdays in our lives were acknowledged with letters or cards that brought laughter or tears... or both. I've saved those letters and cards. I bet Larry did, too.

Well, here's another one, old pal. Wherever you are, I love you, miss you, and celebrate another milestone—with you cheering me on.

We all need cheerleaders in life and in business. In business, cheerleaders are a bit easier to find and replace. If you need more cheerleaders, the best way to find them is to cheer for another business. Better yet, cheer for a few businesses. As you cheer loudly for others, you'll notice your own fan base begin to swell. Your one-man band will soon have a full orchestra of boisterous, supportive friends cheering your every success. Harmony in action!

So get out there and mingle. Join a networking group. You're likely to find some good ones, wherever you live. I'm a member of BNI (Business Network International), and my business and social lives are richer as a result. Check out your local Chamber of Commerce. Find industry-specific associations. And don't just show up—cheer!

*August 11, 2001*

*Tom,*

*As we turn 50 I can think of no better way to describe what we mean to one another than "old friends." Damn good friends at that. Not just good, but the best of friends, with a bond that few men are likely to be blessed with. Our bond goes back probably 45 years thru lots of twists and turns, in and out of school. As children and as men, and of course during those precarious in-between years.*

*Old friends share so many memories, so many rich times. God knows we have them. Memories so rich that I will always cherish them.*

*Old friends understand each other. Who we are, what makes us tick, why we tick the way we do and why sometimes we don't always tick so well.*

*Old friends reach milestones together, cheering on the other, side by side. That's why it's so nice we can be together now as we reach the milestone of our 50th birthdays.*

*Old friends teach each other, as you have taught me, what friendship is all about. What it means to be able to count on another. Tom, you are hands down the most loyal friend I know. I know of no one else like you that would come to my aid regardless of my need. You are an inspiration; a model of friendship unparalleled in my life.*

*And finally, old friends need each other. Because as this old friendship proves, we can make each other better, happier, more successful and more fulfilled together. We improve our lives and the lives of our loved ones together, and best of all we have so much fun, together.*

*Happy Birthday,*
*Larry*

# CHECK AND RECHECK YOUR ASSUMPTIONS

*Never theorize before you have data.*
*Invariably, you end up twisting the facts to suit*
*theories instead of theories to suit facts.*
—Sherlock Holmes

MY FIRST VISION QUEST WAS fifteen years ago, and for nine of the past fifteen summers, I've travelled to Utah to spend time in the wilderness. More than once, I arrived in pretty rough shape, overwhelmed by the stress of my everyday life. The responsibilities of running my business kept me from traveling for a few years, but whenever I did make it out there, the wilderness always welcomed me back.

I look for a spot where I'm not likely to be disturbed, and spend up to a week alone. Generally, up to four of those days are spent fasting and exploring the deeper recesses of my soul. Many of my friends find this ridiculous, but I see it as an opportunity to reconnect with myself, especially after an extended time away from the land that energizes me.

I usually do some hiking before heading out to the great unknown. The trails help me get in tune with the rhythm of the land while I shed the intense energy of business and daily life.

Last summer, I chose to push myself harder than usual and started out with a real whopper: the Grand Canyon rim-to-rim hike. The physical challenge and stunning scenery are trademarks of one of the most dramatic, yet accessible, hikes in the American West.

To prepare, I read books, blogs, and travel guides and spoke with friends who had hiked the trail before. One book mentioned every Grand Canyon death in recorded history, chronicling the incidents by age and sex of hiker, time of year, location in the canyon, and more. I was pretty clear on what I needed to do to survive.

Admittedly, I didn't do the extensive physical preparation recommended throughout the literature, but I figured I was strong or stupid enough to handle the physical challenge. I also purchased a Fitbit to monitor the miles I walked and calories I burned each day. In Dayton, I enjoyed checking how far I walked and got satisfaction from racking up the miles. Looking forward to trails where I knew the distance from start to finish, I figured I could gauge exactly how far I was from my destination.

I chose to hike down the North Kaibab Trail. At 14.3 miles, it is the longest trail into the canyon, and mostly downhill. I planned to stay overnight at Phantom Ranch and head back up via the 9.6-mile Bright Angel Trail the following morning.

I awoke before dawn, rechecked my backpack, and set out for the trailhead. The trail can get extremely hot in July and August, but I love the heat, so I wasn't overly concerned about the forecast. The temperature was expected to reach 107 degrees by early afternoon and up to 120 degrees in "The Box." (More on that later.) I wanted to be at the ranch by noon, and that seemed reasonable.

Insofar as there was really only one way down, the trail was easy to follow. But I brought a map, just in case. I knew where the water stations were and had enough water with me to make it easily from one to the next. I had energy bars, nuts, and emergency gear in case I had to sleep on the trail. I was prepared.

It was barely light and a bit chilly when I set foot on the trail at 5:45 a.m. I did feel some fear, but it was exhilarating rather than debilitating. Although I knew an adventure lay ahead, I was confident I would meet and conquer every challenge encountered on the way down.

I began the journey upbeat and smiling. I was walking a trail in one of the most beautiful places on earth and I was grateful for the gifts that led me to that moment.

Given that most of the literature warns against hiking in the heat of the summer, I didn't expect to encounter much traffic during the first week in August. I was going to have some alone time on the trail. Great!

The first couple miles of the trail dip steeply downhill with few flat areas to give my quads and hamstrings a break. I was prepared for this and took regular breaks to hydrate and rest my muscles.

I was still feeling strong as the sun rose above the canyon. I saw a young couple ahead taking a break and picked up my pace to catch up to them before they got back on the trail. They were familiar with the trail and gave me some pointers about timing, distance, and water. All was well.

Back on the trail after my break, I felt great and was ready for the next leg of the hike. The scenery was incredible, of course, but I was more focused on getting to the bottom, so I didn't spend too much time admiring the views.

As the temperature rose, I found myself paying close attention to my Fitbit and the distance I had travelled. When I passed the eight-mile mark just before nine a.m., I knew I was more than halfway there and anticipated arriving at the ranch before noon. Just as I had planned!

Solo hiking on a well-marked trail is an opportunity to allow the mind to wander. I drifted in and out of thoughts about my business, about what I would do when I reached the ranch, about telling Sam of my Canyon experience, and about whether the Cubs might actually make the postseason that year.

By 11:15 a.m., it was over ninety degrees, and my breaks were becoming more frequent. I had walked thirteen miles, and my pace had slowed a bit. I was still making decent progress, although I was concerned because it didn't seem as though I was just a mile from the ranch. I assumed I was slightly confused from the heat and that I'd see the ranch in the distance soon enough.

By half past noon, I was losing strength rapidly and could take only a few steps without having to rest. I knew the symptoms of hyperthermia and feared I was getting close to the danger zone. Then I reached "The Box."

The Box is an extremely narrow part of the trail. It is an oven in the summer and should not be entered at noon in August. It is also the last part of the longest stretch of the trail without drinking water.

By this point, I was fixated on my Fitbit. It said I had walked more than fifteen miles, yet I was nowhere near the ranch. If I had been more coherent, I would have focused on conserving energy, staying hydrated, and using the few spots of shade to rest, but all I could think about was the blinking number telling me how far I'd walked.

I argued with and cursed the Fitbit. I demanded an explanation from the universe. I pretty much lost control. Despite the extreme heat, I wasn't sweating; neither was I rational enough to take any of the available remedial options to deal with the problem. I knew I was in trouble, but I just kept going.

I felt certain the ranch would appear around each bend, but all I found was more punishing disappointment… sixteen miles… seventeen miles… and still no sign of the ranch. This was supposed to be a fourteen-mile hike! I couldn't turn around; that would not end well. I'd almost given up on finding the ranch, but I continued on, hoping to at least find some shade.

I couldn't take more than one or two steps without stopping to catch my breath. The heat was overwhelming, and there was virtually no shade. My legs were throbbing, and I was afraid to sit, fearing I would be unable to get up.

Could I be lost? I hadn't seen another hiker for hours, and, even if I were on the correct trail, it was highly unlikely that anyone would come through The Box until the next morning. My options were diminishing. And so were my hopes.

Having gone eighteen miles, I had nothing left. I was leaning against a hot rock wall to keep myself upright. One step. Rest. Another step. Rest. I was too delirious to think about dying and too stubborn to quit.

I approached another bend with no expectations. I was just shuffling forward out of habit. I had nothing else to do. Then I caught a glimpse of what appeared to be a signpost about a hundred yards ahead.

After so many imagined ranch sightings, I no longer trusted my vision. This time, though, the sign didn't disappear or turn out to be a shadow from a nearby bush. I was a quarter mile from Phantom Ranch!

Though too tired even to smile, I knew I was safe and would soon be able to lie down in some shade. I began to see people, other hikers who had wisely taken either the South Kaibab or Bright Angel Trail, who were now relaxing, sharing stories of their journey.

I'm sure I looked pretty rough, but nobody seemed to notice. Just another hiker coming through the campground. Before I stopped to rest, I saw a guy with a Fitbit on his wrist.

I got a sudden boost of energy. I needed to know if he, too, had been betrayed by technology. My final reading was exactly nineteen miles. What lie had his Fitbit told?

"I have no idea how many miles it was. I rode down on a donkey," he told me. Perhaps that's why he looked as composed as a guy ready to take his kids to soccer practice. "But I can tell you that these things are never right on mileage," he added. "I just use mine to count calories and monitor my sleep pattern." Oh, really? Apparently I was the only person so pathetically unaware of this key bit of information.

I had done my research before leaving home, preparing for the hike with the same diligence and thoroughness I would have had I been helping a client launch a new business. I had made assumptions based on the best available information and, in the same way I would evaluate business risk, I'd studied the trail and was aware of the dangers of a summer hike. Just as I would determine the expenses required to get a business off the ground, I purchased all the supplies I would need in case of emergency, including water, food, and temporary shelter. I even brought a map and a compass, just in case. I consulted with experts and hikers who had been on this particular trail, in much the same way I would investigate businesses—successful and not-so-successful—in the industry my client was hoping to enter. Yes, I had taken some liberties with my training, but I was confident in my physical condition. Where had I gone wrong? What more could I have done?

The answer is pretty simple, really, and painfully obvious. I *assumed* the Fitbit did all the things the marketing material and advertisements promised. I made no attempt to confirm the manufacturer's claims. I would never allow a client to cut corners like that; I would make sure our assumptions were thoroughly tested and frequently retested.

In my excitement at the prospect of taking this extraordinary hike, I made a mistake that could have had dire consequences. In the heady days of starting a business or planning a daring trip, an extra set of eyes and an unbiased viewpoint can increase the likelihood of your success. If you are planning to hike into a canyon, start a new business, or expand into a new territory, consult experts.

The truth is, I should have had someone check my work. This is what my clients pay me to do—ask the right questions, pay attention to the details, and steer them away from danger. I could have used a trip coach. Don't leave home, or start a business, without one.

# 26

# GRADUATION

*Go confidently in the direction of your dreams.*
—Henry David Thoreau

AT AGE TWENTY-TWO, AFTER THREE laps around senior year, Sam Rubens became a high school graduate. For many kids, high school is really just a place to get their ticket punched on the way to college and whatever comes next.

Not for Sam.

First of all, Sam lives in the present, so "whatever comes next" is not particularly relevant now, since now is where "it" is always "at."

Secondly, Sam's high school experience was about more than books, tests, football games, and proms. High school helped him gain self-confidence, make friends, and have fun with other kids his age. By that measure, his accomplishments were nothing less than valedictorian.

Autistic people come in many varieties, and Sam is roughly in the middle of what is known in the autistic community as "the spectrum." If you ever have the good fortune to meet him, you'll recognize some of his issues—he'll ask you as many questions as you'll tolerate and may comment on your clothes, haircut, or the pimple on your nose—you'll probably be seduced by his infectiously happy personality.

Sam's graduation party gave me an opportunity to observe some of what he had accomplished during six years at Centerville High School.

The party was a simple affair. We had a tent in the front yard—Sam hates the rain, so we had to be prepared! There was the usual picnic food and lawn chairs, with aunts, uncles, and assorted "old people" sitting around talking about this and that while kids wandered in and out foraging for food. Sam was in heaven. He knew everyone and was so excited to introduce the disparate members of his vast fan club to each other.

Sam welcomed every guest with a beaming smile and a huge hug. His demeanor spoke volumes about the comfort he feels in his own skin and projected the joy with which he greets everyone on his journey. When Sam is talking to you, you feel as if you're the most important person in the world. And to Sam, you are.

The guests were the expected assemblage of family, neighbors, fellow graduates, and teachers. What made this gathering unique was the random assortment of "others" in

Sam's sphere. Among the celebrants were the retired janitor from his middle school, a teacher's aide and crossing guard from first grade, and employees from our favorite grocery store. There are no strangers in Sam's world; everyone is his friend.

The joy Sam brings to the lives of his friends is evident in the way they light up the moment they see him. For Sam, having fun is a choice he makes every day. And that is contagious.

In his remarkable commencement speech at Stanford in 2007—which you can watch on YouTube, if you haven't seen it—the late Steve Jobs spoke of connecting the dots in life. "You can't connect the dots looking forward; you can only connect them looking backward. So you have to trust that the dots will somehow connect in your future. You have to trust in something—your gut, destiny, life, karma, whatever. This approach has never let me down, and it has made all the difference in my life."

Seen from that perspective, graduation is the opportunity to look back and connect another dot, while celebrating the exhilaration of anticipation as you journey forth to the unknown, to all the dots you will connect in the years to come.

When you think about it, isn't every day a graduation, giving us the opportunity to acknowledge past successes and look forward to future accomplishments and milestones? The dots that challenge us become turning points that shape the heroic journey we are all traveling at this very moment.

We can sustain the excitement of our graduation by remembering that the life we are creating is always cause for celebration. When you can't see the next dot on the horizon, look back and see how far you've come, and trust, as Jobs said, "in your gut, destiny, life, karma, whatever."

For many people, graduation also represents crossing the threshold into adulthood. Jobs, family, and careers await.

As my favorite human being passed another milestone on his journey, I recognized that we all have more dots to connect. And like the ones that came before, they will be all the right dots. The journey continues.

# FINAL THOUGHTS

*All I know is that my life is better when I
assume that people are doing their best.
It keeps me out of judgment and lets me focus
on what is, and not what should or could be.*
—Brené Brown

ASSUMING OTHERS ARE DOING THEIR best is one my favorite ways to find harmony. I've used it on the highway, when I'm behind someone in the left lane texting away without even a glance in his rearview mirror. It has come in handy when I'm stuck behind a person in the grocery store who thought twenty-nine was less than ten, as in, "ten items or less in this lane, please." If I'm sounding like an impatient person, that's because I am. Please assume I'm doing my best.

My "aha" harmony moment came a few years ago at a wilderness retreat in Colorado. We were gathered to learn about the art of mirroring, which I now use every day, and the way of council. There were about twenty-five of us gathered in a circle when I made an astounding observation.

I don't know about you, but I find that most groups of that size tend to have a similar archetypal makeup. Of course, there's the narcissist, it's all about him. There's the woman who knows everything about everything and can't wait to enlighten you. There's the most interesting man in the world, the guy all the women want to date and the men want to be. You probably have your own set of archetypes that show up at your events.

At some point, after a couple of days together, I looked around and noticed that one familiar archetype was missing. This guy was pretty much a regular in my world. I couldn't remember another group I'd been a part of where he failed to show up. But this time he was nowhere to be found. Nope. There were no assholes in this group.

When I realized he was missing, I immediately also understood why. I had changed. The reason the asshole hadn't shown up was because that part of me was no longer omnipresent. His visits were less frequent as I progressed on my journey. He still shows up occasionally, sure. But seeking harmony and assuming the best in others is the surest way I've found to keep his appearances at a minimum. It will do the same for you, if you let it.

Earlier, I asked for your indulgence as I redefined "*lifeness*" as "The state or quality of having a life in which personal and business goals are harmoniously merged to maximize the joy and abundance derived from each."

I hope you feel ready to reengineer your life and business to achieve the *lifeness* you seek. The next time your Loyal Soldier pops up, you two can harmonize rather than argue. Fear, your newest ally, is now at your side as a guard against the pain of regret. With harmony as your barometer, the measure of your success will be the number of situations in your life and work in which dissonance evaporates in benign resignation.

In your quest to endure and thrive as a leader, your Pillars of Truth will keep your compass pointed toward harmony. You have a plan, a mission, and a vision to uphold as you create a culture grounded in the desire for harmony in all aspects of your life.

I'm honored that your journey led you to this book, and I hope you now feel better equipped to experience *lifeness*. The mere fact that you found this book and finished it tells me that you're primed to reach for the highest fruit. I want to see you squeeze every bit of juice out of this life.

In order to help you do that, I've created *The Lifeness Journal*. It comes with exciting new tools to guide you toward more days of harmonic inspiration.

You can go to www.LifenessJournal.com to learn more and order your copy. At www.TomRubens.com, you'll find information about our Facebook group, masterminds, and the latest goodies for our tribe.

You can reach me at Tom@TomRubens.com. Keep in touch. I'd love to hear about your *lifeness*, and the harmony you're creating.

# ACKNOWLEDGMENTS

WHILE WRITING A BOOK MAY be seen by some as a solitary pursuit, it is truly a collaborative endeavor. In this, my first book, I have been fortunate to have abundant assistance.

My extraordinarily supportive Miracle Morning/BNI group, Becky Edgren, Andrea Porter, John Highley, Shelagh McGovern, Jeff Blumer, Mike Smith, Cindy Gaboury, Janice Bretelson, Gary Hardy, Dan Cleary, and Tony Harker, steadfastly encouraged me, while Jane Fiehrer, our collective conscience and resident intuitive, gave me no alternative but to keep writing until a book emerged.

When I thought I was ready to go to print, I reached out to AJ Harper for help with a companion piece I planned to write. She quickly nixed that idea and gently suggested that what I thought was a finished product was in need of more work. Her steadfast refusal to accept anything less than my best writing helped me to find the book hidden amongst the words I'd written.

CB Messer, with very little input from me, created a cover that is a perfect visual expression of the words I wrote. She also did the typesetting, and responded warmly to my frequent "last minute absolutely final" changes. CB is a graceful woman of many talents.

Fellow coaches Amber Vilhauer, Bruce D Schneider, Jay Meyer, Dave Dudon, and Bob Corcoran were all gracious with both their time and their insights.

David Homan introduced me to McGohan Brabender and the Keeper of the Culture, Scott Mcgowan. I am deeply indebted to each of them for allowing me inside their remarkable company.

My current and past clients have taught me far more than they realize, and I am so grateful for the confidence they have shown in me and the friendships we have created.

I love to write and tell stories, but punctuation and sentence structure have never been my strong suit. Tom Gelli did his best to keep me from the shameful misuse of commas, semicolons, and ellipses. Zoe Bird and Nicki Harper further cleaned up my punctuation, while delicately offering tips to clarify my message. Sometimes, I actually took their suggestions.

My dear friend, Frances Duncan has been my writing coach, confidante, and chief butt-kicker from start to finish. Without her, this book would not exist.